Vaccine Guide
for *Dogs* and *Cats*

What Every Pet Lover
Should Know

By Catherine J. M. Diodati, M.A.

New Atlantean Press
Santa Fe, New Mexico

Vaccine Guide
for *Dogs* and *Cats*
What Every Pet Lover
Should Know

By Catherine J. M. Diodati, M.A.

International Standard Book Number:
1-881217-34-5
Library of Congress Catalog Card Number:
2003007250

Library of Congress Cataloging-in-Publication Data

Diodati, Catherine, 1959-
    Vaccine guide for dogs and cats : what every pet lover should know /
by Catherine J.M. Diodati.
        p. cm.
Includes bibliographical references (p. 113).
    ISBN 1-881217-34-5 (pbk.)
    1. Dogs–Diseases. 2. Cats–Diseases. 3. Veterinary vaccines.
    4. Vaccination of animals. I. Title.
        SF991.D56 2003
        636.7'0896–dc21

                        2003007250

Printed in the United States of America

Published by:
New Atlantean Press
PO Box 9638
Santa Fe, NM 87504

www.thinktwice.com

What Others Are Saying:

"My experiences have brought me to the conclusion that vaccines are more of a factor in the production of chronic disease in our animals than we have ever anticipated. Veterinarians and pet lovers alike have long needed the information that Catherine Diodati has gathered for us in this book. It is a real gift. Diodati provides us with a comprehensive picture of vaccines—their development and use—enabling us to think more seriously about this practice. Before this book, we did not know the facts. Ms. Diodati has given us the tools we need to consider this issue intelligently."

—Richard Pitcairn, DVM, PhD, Director, Animal Natural Health Center; Author, *Dr. Pitcairn's Complete Guide to Natural Health for Dogs and Cats*

"A universal [vaccination] scheme cannot be expected to accommodate the immunology of the carnivore, the properties of diverse infectious agents, the changing epidemiologic situation, or the age and living environment of the animal. Injection and immunization are not synonymous. The automatic yearly application of a polyvalent preparation [multiple vaccination] with disregard for the vaccinee's individual life circumstances is a dangerous development."

—American Animal Hospital Association (AAHA)

"Finally, an educational resource on the problems with 'preventive' medicine! Over the past twenty years the overall health of animals has deteriorated. For example, dogs were much healthier prior to 1980. We had problems with distemper and parvo before vaccines, but now we have the same problems plus many more, including autoimmune ailments, neurological afflictions, learning disorders, canine autism, rage syndrome, eye and skin disease, inflammatory joint problems, urinary tract infections, alopecia, anorexia, fatigue, and more.

"You don't have to be a rocket scientist to figure out why drug companies deny vaccine reactions. A special thanks to Catherine Diodati and all the vets who recognize that there are problems with preventive medicine. This book will educate the public. Hopefully, our cats will purr once more and our dogs will start wagging their tails again."

—Darla Lofranco, Professional Animal Breeder, 30 years

To my Ashleigh and to my Angel.
Thank you for more than words can express.

Acknowledgments

First and foremost I must acknowledge the support and assistance of my family. I love them dearly and appreciate their patience while I have been away heavily focused on my research and writing. In particular, my beautiful daughter Ashleigh has made many sacrifices to assist me. Thank you, my love. Seventeen years ago, Ashleigh opened my eyes to the dangers associated with vaccination. At six months of age, she suffered a nearly fatal reaction thus initiating my life's quest.

I would also like to extend my most sincere appreciation to Nathan Wright of New Atlantean Press. It was Nathan who first envisioned this book and approached me to write it. I truly appreciate his patience, support and kindness.

Thank you to David Hull of the Ontario Veterinary College Library for his generous assistance. Thank you to the University of Windsor's Leddy Library staff who continue to allow me to access the ILL program. Without this kind courtesy, I would surely have spent many more weeks in hotels exploring Canadian and U.S. veterinary libraries.

Thank you to Dr. F. Edward Yazbak, MD, FAAP for his contributions and insight. Dr. Yazbak's research on the effects of MMR vaccination around gestation, pregnancy, and during breastfeeding, not only provided significant implications for this book but will ultimately protect many children. It has been my great privilege to work with Dr. Yazbak to discover correlations between the distemper and measles vaccines and serious adverse events to offspring. Thank you to Linda Hodgdon, author of *Visual Strategies for Improving Communication* and *Solving Behaviour Problems in Autism*, for sharing her insights on behaviors associated with autism.

Many thanks to Doctors Patty Smith and Rudi Verspoor, of the Hahnemann Center Clinic in Ottawa, Ontario, for generously allowing me access to their library and for providing consultation on homeopathy. Thank you to Dr. Susan Beal, of Big Run Healing Arts, Big Run PA, for kindly sharing her expertise. Thank you to Dr. Richard Bray, DC, for the many wonderful adjustments that allowed me to spend hours poring over books and on the computer. I can't imagine having done this work without his help.

I wish to thank Dr. Harash Narang, of the CJD Foundation, for kindly sharing his expertise and references regarding formaldehyde and foot-and-mouth disease. Thank you to the many scientists and authors internationally who kindly shared their research and willingly answered my questions. In particular, I would like to recognize the assistance of Dr. Bob Friendship, Dr. Linn A. Wilbur, Dr. Martin Goldstein, Dr. Dean H. Percy, and Dr. Virginia Studdert. Special thanks to Sheri Nakken and Dawn Richardson for their very kind assistance.

A huge debt of gratitude goes to Rudy Moralez, Jr. While completing this book, he helped me clear several computer viruses that could have eliminated over two years' worth of research. Many, many thanks—I am so very grateful for his help and support.

Many thanks to my dear friend Edda West, co-founder of the Vaccination Risk Awareness Network for her help and support. Because of her work, many lives have been saved and the rights of others have been protected. I would like to thank Alan Yurko for providing a number of resources. Alan currently resides in a Florida State prison because he was wrongfully convicted of murdering his infant son. Having thoroughly reviewed Alan's case, I am unequivocally convinced that his son did not die from Shaken Baby Syndrome but died due to vaccine injuries. I pray for his release and for a growing awareness that will prevent such injuries and halt similar wrongful accusations and convictions.

A great debt of thanks goes to Marguerite Wegner, founder of the Rabbit Information Service in Riverton, Western Australia, for her assistance and generosity. Many thanks to Darla Lofranco, an Acton Ontario Kuvasz Breeder, for generously sharing her experiences and for the efforts she is making to protect dogs from the adverse effects of drugs and vaccines. Thank you to Kathy Goyeau, of Groom at the Top, Professional Dog Grooming, Windsor, Ontario, for kindly taking the time for a consultation during an extremely busy period. Thank you to the many pet owners and breeders, particularly the members of *Just Say No To Vaccines*, who kindly shared their experiences with me and patiently provided medical histories over a series of correspondences.

Finally, I would like to thank the many people who have provided assistance, shown interest, and offered guidance throughout this project. This includes my dear friends at Windsor Toastmasters. To them, I extend my heartfelt gratitude for their interest, support, questions, humor, and companionship. They enrich my life.

Disclaimer

TABLE OF CONTENTS

Foreword

Richard Pitcairn, DVM, PhD

For much of my professional career, I perceived vaccines as both beneficial and harmless. I never considered that they could contribute in any way to more subtle and persistent health problems. Yet, the casual practice of yearly vaccinations is now seen by some veterinarians, myself included, as a significant contributor to the striking increase of chronic diseases observed during recent decades.

It might be helpful to explain how *I* came to this conclusion. In 1965, I graduated from veterinary school, University of California at Davis. In my first years in practice we did vaccinate dogs and cats, but much less often than is done today. The standard practice was to give puppy or kitten shots at the ages of eight weeks and twelve weeks. This was all that was done until another year went by and then one booster was given. Except for rabies, that was it. It was understood that these vaccines, if they did their job, would protect for the life of the animal. I still remember when an article first appeared suggesting that *perhaps* some of the older dogs, ones that had been isolated in backyards for most of their lives, might have lost immunity. Though there was no real evidence for this, the idea caught on, and soon veterinarians were recommending boosters in these older animals. It did not take long before this practice extended into the *yearly* booster. Also, during the 1960s vaccines were simpler—usually two or three different disease agents were included. Today, many more disease agents are packed into the same shot.

It is difficult for me to understand how such a cavalier attitude could have existed among both veterinarians and the public. We all know that novel biological techniques can have unforeseen consequences and, indeed, this seems to be a common outcome of new medical procedures. Nonetheless, it was commonly assumed that there could be no harm from this practice, and that it was effective at preventing disease. Neither of these assumptions had scientific support. One would hear the practice justified by veterinarians because it would bring clients in for yearly exams. In other words, the yearly vaccine, perhaps not entirely necessary, would still bring about good because the veterinarian would see the animal more often and catch developing problems. Not a bad idea, but hardly establishing a scientific basis for the practice.

My career path took me to graduate school at Washington State University School of Veterinary Medicine. There I studied for a doctorate degree in immunology—the science of the immune system and its functions, including its response to vaccinations. Little attention, if any, was given to the possible harmful effects of vaccines. Indeed, the practice of vaccination was presented as a major triumph of modern medicine. After all, what could be better than something that prevented disease and was completely harmless as well?

This was the attitude that I carried with me from graduate school into private practice. However, in 1978 I began to study homeopathic medicine and applied it to animal treatment. (Homeopathy is a fascinating topic, one that has great promise as an alternative to vaccination.) Slowly and reluctantly I began to question my prior beliefs about vaccines. Several animals that I had toiled over with homeopathic and nutritional therapy became well until they received their yearly boosters and then fell apart. I was able to discount a few of these occurrences, but as this happened more and more often I realized that vaccines were not as neutral and harmless as I originally thought. Next, I started to recognize that some of the symptoms I was seeing in my animals with allergies and other chronic diseases were like the natural diseases for which vaccines were being used. I was convinced that the vaccines were actually contributing to the illnesses that were so common and frustrating for both practitioners and their clients. The vaccines were producing many of the symptoms.

This is not to say that every animal becomes ill after vaccinations. This is clearly not so. However, there are some animals—probably predisposed because of a weak immune system—that cannot handle certain vaccines and become chronically ill as a result of their use.

If I am right about this, why should it be so? How can a vaccine make an animal sick? I don't know the complete answer to this, but I believe that in some cases the vaccine may not be properly attenuated. There is another aspect necessary to understand. When we give a vaccine, which is the disease agent in a weakened form, the idea is that the immune system will react to it by developing immunity. But what if the immune system cannot do this? What if it is not capable of mounting a proper response because of prior health factors? I think that this is certainly the reason in many of the animals I work with. Often they have not had a good start, either not developing well or showing signs of allergies or other immune problems early in life. If we realize that an allergic state is one in which the immune system is already acting inappropriately, we can see how asking it to react to a complex vaccine injection may just be adding fuel to the fire.

Over the years, vaccines have also become more complex. There are more of them used, many different types, and each may contain numerous viruses and germs—five, six, or more. The immune systems of some animals may become confused by all this information. For example, the immune system acts in a way similar to our memory. It recognizes foreign material and then stores the memory of the encounter. In the same way that our memory can be confused by too much information coming in at the same time, I believe the immune system can be confused by the overwhelming material it encounters after a vaccination. It is hardly a natural process for five or six disease agents to end up in an animal's bloodstream simultaneously, but this is what happens when a vaccine injection is given. Too much, too fast.

My experiences have brought me to the conclusion that vaccines are more of a factor in the production of chronic disease in our animals than we have ever anticipated. Veterinarians and pet lovers alike have long needed the information that Catherine Diodati has gathered for us in this book. It is a real gift. Diodati provides us with a comprehensive picture of vaccines—their development and use—enabling us to think more seriously about this practice. Before this book, we did not know the facts. Ms. Diodati has given us the tools we need to consider this issue intelligently.

Richard Pitcairn, DVM, PhD
Director, Animal Natural Health Center
Author, *Dr. Pitcairn's Complete Guide to Natural Health for Dogs and Cats*

Preface

We have been paying well-intentioned people to administer toxic and carcinogenic substances to our pets—sometimes damaging or killing them—hoping to prevent diseases which may never occur. Sadly, more ignorance than knowledge surrounds vaccination. It is precisely this lack of knowledge that stands behind the annual revaccination of our pets. We are needlessly over-vaccinating them, repeatedly exposing our canines and felines to multiple pathogens and dangerous chemicals. This makes them unduly susceptible to the very ailments we hope to prevent. They become prone to disease-related complications and degenerative disorders as well.

Many veterinarians, both allopathic and holistic, are questioning the validity of annual revaccination. They are moving away from this arbitrary recommendation. Many also refuse to use certain vaccines because the disease in question is either so innocuous or rare that the risks associated with vaccination outweigh any promised benefit. They understand that repeatedly injecting unnecessary vaccines is harming their animal clients. Some veterinarians have designed reduced vaccination schedules, using only a few monovalent (single) vaccines and insisting on an interval of weeks between administering others. They have also learned that vaccination must be avoided in sick animals—no matter how mild the illness appears—and in animals who are otherwise stressed, on medication, or have received surgery recently.

We make the best decisions we can with the information we have. For far too long, accurate vaccine information has not reached our hands, and our pets are paying dearly. Many veterinary vaccines are either safe *or* effective; more often they are neither. Would you *knowingly* choose to vaccinate your dog against coronavirus if you knew that the disease is extremely rare, very mild, and that the vaccine elicited questionable immunity yet causes a variety of serious adverse events, including meningitis and death? Would you *knowingly* vaccinate your indoor cat, who will not be exposed to many diseases, with vaccines known to cause cancer? Of course not. Nevertheless, we have been making vaccination decisions with limited access to accurate information.

My interest in veterinary vaccines arose from my own experiences with pets over the years. I watched diabetes develop in one dog and a large cyst develop in another at the site typically used for vaccination. I also observed a cat become rapidly ill and die without any other plausible explanation. I wondered about a vaccine connection in each case. Having researched human vaccines for many years (i.e., *Immunization: History, Ethics, Law and Health*), I am quite aware of a vast array of vaccine-induced adverse events. I travel frequently, giving professional and lay presentations on vaccination. Invariably there are members in the audience who ask questions about veterinary vaccines or share stories of how veterinary vaccines have affected their pets or livestock. So, when New Atlantean Press approached me to write this book, I was more than a little intrigued by the prospect. What I have found over the past few years of research is that veterinary vaccines carry exactly the same risks and efficacy problems as human vaccines. We should approach them with the same caution and skepticism.

It is my sincere hope that this book will provide you with enough information to make informed decisions for your animal clients and/or cherished pets.

Catherine J. M. Diodati, MA

Introduction

Vaccinations are given to prevent disease. Yet, despite these medical "advancements" and the veterinary industry's sincere desire to explore new ways to improve health, our pets are becoming more and more ill. Cancer, diabetes, tumors, seizures, digestive problems, organ failure, arthritis and a host of other ailments are no longer reserved for aging animals; they are afflicting very young pets as well, and reducing their life expectancies. Although there are a number of factors that can contribute to this pervasive decline in wellness, such as diet and drugs, with every vaccine that we allow our beloved pets to receive, we are subjecting them to viruses, bacteria, and toxic chemicals. How can we inject dangerous substances into their bloodstreams and expect improved health?

Although we have been using vaccines for more than two centuries, there is still a great deal that we do not know about their safety, efficacy, and duration of immunity. In fact, we are still trying to understand how the immune system functions. A lot of what we do know about immunity was discovered in the past 40 years. Until recently, the science of immunity focused almost entirely on the type and quantity of antibodies directed against specific pathogens. While antibodies are important, they represent just one facet of a vast, and necessarily interdependent, network. We now know that other key elements are required in order to evoke an efficient immune response.

When a pathogen is encountered naturally, the first line of immune defenses are activated, usually involving the skin, gastro-intestinal tract, or mucous membranes. More often than not, germs are defeated long before they can even cause symptoms. When an infection does progress, very specific immune cells are activated ensuring that the unwelcome pathogen is correctly identified. Next, they confront the pathogen limiting its ability to reproduce and infect cells. They also respond by destroying and removing the pathogen from the body. Once the invader has been defeated, memory cells remain alert in case the same pathogen is encountered again. This protection also extends to future generations via natural passive

15

immunity conferred through the womb and breastmilk.

Vaccine-induced immunity functions differently. Pathogens, plus vaccine chemicals, bypass the normal route of entry and are introduced directly into the bloodstream. The body is left scrambling to mount an effective immune response. Dr. Harold Buttram, vaccine researcher, theorized that this type of surprise attack may burden the immune system ten times greater than a natural infection.[1] It is also important to note that natural infections help to mature the immune system. By reducing *natural* challenges, and increasing *artificial* exposures to pathogens and toxic chemicals, we are creating generations with a greater susceptibility to infections, allergies, autoimmune ailments, cancer and a variety of degenerative diseases.[2]

There are also important differences between the duration of immunity induced by natural versus artificial means. Although there are a few exceptions, natural infection generally results in permanent immunity whereas vaccine-induced immunity is temporary, lasting anywhere from a few months to a few years. Natural immunity also provides passive immunity to offspring, protecting them from disease for a critical period after birth and while nursing. Some immunity will be transferred through the placenta. Much of it is also derived through colostrum.[3] On the other hand, because vaccine-induced immunity, when it is elicited, wanes over time, often it will not provide sufficient protection for both the mother and her offspring.[4]

Passive immunity is important, not only for current generations, but for future ones as well. When a disease enters a species for the first time, its results are frequently devastating. Survivors provide passive immunity to their offspring, who are then better equipped to mount an immune response to the disease. At the same time, the pathogen will adapt, or mutate, so that it does not destroy its required host. Over time, due to the natural host-pathogen interaction, the disease becomes less of a threat. Morbidity (the incidence of disease) and mortality decline significantly.

The importance of natural passive immunity was well-demonstrated in 1950 when a deadly myxoma virus was purposely introduced into the Australian wild rabbit population because they were threatening agricultural interests.[5] At first, the virus proved lethal to most rabbits. Over time, however, the survivors became more resistant to the virus and within a few years the rabbit population again grew to its original size. The surviving rabbits had developed immunity through a series of exposures and provided passive immunity to their offspring, creating a population *resistant* to myxoma virus. Simultaneously, the virus mutated and the spring influx of new mosquitos spread less virulent strains of myxoma. The antigen-host relationship tends to favor coexistence: a lethal pathogen will become less virulent as a more resistant host emerges.[6] The natural evolutionary process typically continues in this manner until the disease presents little threat to future generations. When we interfere with this process through vaccination, we are robbing future generations of the benefits natural passive immunity provides.

Vaccine technology is trying to catch up to new discoveries, yet remains powerless to guarantee safe and effective results. Vaccines are often unable to provide adequate protection against disease, and frequently result in unexpected, detrimental consequences. For example, any vaccine can cause an immediate, and potentially fatal, allergic/anaphylactic reaction. Peanut, a 12-year-old Dachshund, was fortunate to have survived such a reaction. Almost immediately after vaccination, her eyes and mouth began swelling; soon her body swelled, and she had difficulty breathing. Since she was vaccinated during a house call, and the veterinarian had already left, she was brought into an emergency clinic for a shot of epinephrine (adrenalin). Her reaction could have been fatal if it was not recognized and treated so quickly.

Scarlett, a 4½-year-old domestic cat, also had a serious reaction to her shot. An hour after vaccination, she was found under a table, breathing sporadically, unable to lift her head. Scarlett had emptied her bowels and bladder, and was now moaning softly and drooling. Scarlett spent the next few days at the veterinarian's office where they said she was reacting to the rabies portion of the combination vaccine. Scarlett took another full week to recover. She is now much quieter, does not play very much, and has one eye that remains lazy. Strangely, the veterinarian did not blame the vaccine for the reaction; he faulted the cat for being sensitive to it. Since this time, Scarlett has had two other veterinarians attending her. The first insisted upon booster vaccines despite the fact that her reaction contraindicated them. The second veterinarian listened and knew better than to further compromise her life. (Her owner received a bill for several hundred dollars to treat Scarlett's vaccine reaction. She refused to pay, and rightly so, since it was the medical intervention that caused the problem in the first place.)

Some vaccine reactions take longer to appear. Seizures, for example, commonly arise a few days to a few weeks following vaccination. Belle and Beau, sibling Rat terriers, both had serious vaccine side effects that took somewhat different forms. Belle had an immediate reaction: she shrieked in pain, her eyes swelled shut, and she spent the first night shivering. Within 24 hours Belle recovered. Her brother Beau, on the other hand, did not react immediately but soon began vomiting and having seizures. Beau's seizures persisted until all vaccines were stopped. Both dogs developed deformities and rotting teeth. Although one might consider their diet or genetics responsible for this, none of their puppies have had similar problems.

In some cases, an initial reaction is clear but the full impact is not immediately evident. Waylon, a Brindle Great Dane, received his second vaccination series at 3½ months of age, a combined booster plus rabies vaccines. Waylon immediately became excessively sleepy, refused to eat, and developed a high temperature. Other changes, however, did not become evident until the initial reactions subsided. Prior to vaccination, Waylon was "a loving little pup who would gaze into [your] eyes and just cuddle and snuggle." After vaccination, his eyes had a glazed look, he no longer made eye contact, and would not tolerate physical contact. Much like the vaccine-induced autism witnessed in children, it was difficult to hold Waylon's attention or to distract him away from repetitive or destructive behaviors. He began destroying his bedding and a stuffed doll that he used to carry everywhere, cuddle with, and treat gently. He also started running nonstop until his owner could bribe him to come into the house; then he would dash about in the house as well. Fortunately, Waylon has improved considerably with the help of a good homeopathic protocol.

Other reactions can take even longer to manifest, such as injection-site tumors, diabetes, arthritis, and a variety of autoimmune disorders. Many of these conditions, and their treatments, are far worse than the diseases we are trying to prevent through vaccination. For example, Brandy, an English springer spaniel, developed autoimmune hemolytic anemia (destruction of oxygen-carrying red blood cells) within a few weeks of receiving a rabies vaccine when he was 4½ years old. Brandy was placed on Prednisone to treat the condition and developed diabetes from the drug. Brandy then developed cataracts and his impaired vision led to the loss of an eye. He lost one toe to cancer and suffers from bladder infections because the diabetes is so difficult to control. There has been a cascade effect on Brandy's health that stems directly from vaccination. Would he have ever even been exposed to rabies? There is no question that this dog's life has been radically changed in order to prevent something that may never have occurred in the first place.

Stress, Environment and Immune Function

The immune system is remarkable in its ability to fend off disease and promote recovery. However, stress and environmental factors exert enormous effects on the immune system's response to disease or vaccines. If, for example, an animal succumbs to two pathogens simultaneously, it will be ill for a longer period than if only one pathogen is encountered.[7] Similarly, vaccinating during illness, no matter how mild the ailment may appear, is completely inadvisable because the animal's immune system is already addressing one challenge and should not be further challenged. Vaccination is well-known to amplify what otherwise might have remained a subclinical or mild infection.[8] Furthermore, an animal that has exhibited a prior vaccine reaction will tend to have more pronounced reactions upon revaccination.

Midas, a 12 year old Labrador retriever, reacted to his first set of vaccines within a few hours. He developed hives all over his body and began running and crashing into walls. His veterinarian stated that this could not be a vaccine reaction, so Midas received further vaccines. Nine months later, a few hours after receiving his booster shots, Midas had his first seizure. He experienced 11 seizures in that first year alone. Shortly thereafter, he began having severe allergy problems and a series of recurrent staph infections. Over the next four years, Midas received annual parvovirus and rabies vaccines. Recently, he was diagnosed with squamous cell (malignant) cancer. Midas also suffers from arthritis and has numerous signs consistent with hypothyroidism. Midas' immune system was over-challenged and has become severely compromised.

Pets who are ill, who have recently received surgery, or who have been exposed to pesticides, antibiotics, or anti-parasitic medications are more susceptible to infection and are at greater risk of adverse vaccine reactions. In some areas, prior to receiving an adopted pet from the local Humane Society or shelter, the pet must first be vaccinated and neutered or spayed. Bombarding the animal's body with so many serious challenges at once may be convenient for humans but it cannot improve the pet's health. Noël, a healthy four-month-old cat, was adopted from the Humane Society. However, after undergoing the required spaying, de-worming, and vaccination, the cat succumbed to a severe respiratory illness and continued wheezing for the remainder of her life. She died at six years of age exhibiting signs of stomach distension, anorexia, wasting, convulsions and heart failure. Noël had consistently remained indoors and was never in contact with other cats after her adoption. Spacing medications, surgery, and vaccination will most assuredly reduce unfavorable outcomes and improve life-expectancy.

In a similar fashion, breeders typically administer certain drugs to their puppies that may have significant detrimental effects. Quite often, breeders will begin the combined vaccination series at four weeks of age, with revaccination occurring every two weeks until the puppies reach 12 weeks of age. This intensive regimen over-burdens the puppies' immature immune systems. Combining vaccination with commonly used anti-protozoal drugs can result in brain and spine lesions, seizures, and other neurological signs. Darla Lofranco, an Ontario Kuvasz breeder, reported severe neurological problems in her puppies following the use of anti-protozoal drugs which were exacerbated by vaccination.[9] The dogs were unable to stand or walk, appeared stunned, were unteachable, had brain and spine lesions, and their eyes and joints were grossly swelled. In each case, vaccinated puppies fared far worse than their unvaccinated counterparts. The anti-protozoal drug used was Amprolium, which induces vitamin B_1 (thiamine) deficiency. Thiamine deficiency is associated with cerebrocortical necrosis (lesions), gastrointestinal and circulation problems, and inability to properly metabolize sugar, among other things. Vaccines, all on their own, can create such adverse effects, so when they are administered to an animal experiencing vitamin B_1 deficiency, the probability of vaccine-induced adverse events is increased significantly.[10] When an alternate anti-protozoal drug (Septra) was tried, other unfavorable reactions were noted.[11] The puppies became quite ill and experienced elevated temperatures, severe alopecia (balding), sudden painful swelling of the lymph nodes, sinus tracts, lips, ears and eyelids. As their faces swelled, draining, crusted sores appeared. Lofranco advises other breeders against vaccinating puppies too early or revaccinating puppies who have demonstrated prior reactions, and using extreme caution when selecting vaccines, antibiotics, and anti-protozoal drugs.

The immune system can be affected by a variety of factors such as nutrition, hygiene, living conditions, extreme temperatures, age and general well-being. All too often, our new pets are exposed to conditions that adversely affect their health. Over-crowding in shelters, pet shops, or kennels not only increases their chances of exposure to various pathogens but makes the animals more susceptible to infection due to the added stress of their environment. Inadequate nutrition and unhygienic conditions similarly compromise the immune system and increase susceptibility to infection.

Free-roaming animals will be exposed to more diseases than indoor animals, and multiple-pet environments pose more risks than single-pet environments. Certain breeds may be more predisposed to certain infections or serious consequences than other breeds. Doberman pinschers, black Labs and Rottweilers, for example, tend to suffer more severe parvovirus manifestations than other breeds.

Generally speaking, very young animals are at greater risk of disease-related complications than adolescent or adult animals. A disease that may be largely inconsequential to an older animal can be fatal in neonates and young animals. Passive, maternally-derived immunity will generally persist for about 12-16 weeks in many pets. As long as maternal antibodies are present in sufficient strength, vaccines are virtually useless during this period. There exists a "window of vulnerability," however, when passive immunity is still strong enough to block any potential immune response to vaccination but is too weak to protect the young animal from infection.[12] The care and environment provided during the early weeks of an animal's life, therefore, are particularly important. Positive efforts should be made to avoid the stresses and exposures that will compromise the health of the animal at any stage of life.

Estrus, Pregnancy, and Lactation

Vaccinating animals during estrus, pregnancy or lactation is extremely risky and should be avoided. Dr. F. Edward Yazbak, pediatrician and vaccine researcher, notes that "hormonal changes can trigger autoimmune disease and, for this reason, it is wise to avoid giving vaccinations [30 days] before, during, or immediately after [the] estrus period."[13] Vaccination during pregnancy can result in serious adverse events to the mother and the fetus, including spontaneous abortion and birth defects. Risks are increased when modified live vaccines are administered. For example, a pregnant queen was vaccinated against parvovirus at the end of her first or beginning of her second trimester of pregnancy and gave birth six weeks later.[14] Of the five kittens born, three died shortly after birth. There was severe hydrocephalus, as well as a lack of cerebellar development, in the remaining two kittens. By eight weeks of age, neither kitten could walk nor had normal functional responses.[15] Parvoviral DNA attributed to the vaccine was found in brain samples of both kittens. The vaccine virus was also found in the kidney of one of the kittens. Similarly, vaccinating a lactating animal can present untenable risks (i.e. the vaccine passing through breastmilk) to the neonates and should be avoided.[16]

Arbitrary Vaccine Mandates

Excluding rabies vaccine mandates, veterinary vaccine schedules are not rigidly standardized (nor legally required) in the same way as human vaccine timetables. This presents an advantage for pets that is virtually ignored in the field of human vaccine use. At least insofar as official recommendations are concerned, there appears to be greater flexibility in considering individual circumstances. For example, recommendations may be quite different for cats who reside indoors than for those who roam outdoors freely and may be exposed to more pathogens. Similarly, certain diseases will be endemic to one area of a country, but not to another, which will affect vaccine recommendations. Recommendations made by manufacturers do not weigh individual circumstances so they should not be considered appropriate for every pet.

Vaccine recommendations have recently come under significant scrutiny from within the veterinary profession. Many vaccine package inserts, which are used to determine both the required dosage and recommended vaccination schedules, typically endorse annual revaccination after the initial series. *Annual revaccination is completely arbitrary, unsupported by science.* In fact, a recent study demonstrated that protective immunity from some canine vaccines endures for at least three years and possibly as long as 15 years.[17] The immunity elicited by some feline vaccines was shown to last for at least three years and possibly seven years or more.[18] Although vaccine manufacturers are now required to provide data regarding the *minimum* duration of immunity for newly developed vaccines; there are no regulations requiring investigation into the *maximum* or *actual* duration of immunity.[19] In most cases, experimental animals are killed after a prescribed number of weeks or months, so a vaccine is said to provide immunity for whatever period of time the experimental animals were allowed to survive. Revaccination recommendations are made based upon the available data. Is it really necessary to revaccinate your pet every year? In most cases, the experts have no scientifically defensible answer.

According to the American Animal Hospital Association (AAHA), "many veterinarians are under the misconception that current recommendations were and are scientifically based when, in fact, they may have less basis than the arguments for change."[20] In response to the profession's demands for simple, commercially attractive vaccination schedules, manufacturers have developed polyvalent (multiple) vaccines to be administered annually.

> The small animal scene gradually adopted a yearly vaccination routine and everybody appeared satisfied: the vet, the owner, the manufacturer. One visit per client per year, one injection, one vaccine—easy enough. In biological terms this is nonsense, of course. A universal scheme cannot be expected to accommodate the immunology of the carnivore, the properties of diverse infectious agents, the changing epidemiologic situation, or the age and living environment (risks of infection) of the animal.
>
> Injection and immunization are not synonymous. The automatic yearly application of a polyvalent preparation with disregard for the vaccinee's individual life circumstances is [a] dangerous development.... It may be damaging for the profession.[21]

The AAHA recognizes the gravity of a vaccination regimen based more upon tradition than sound science. They "encourage appropriate government agencies to include duration of immunity studies as a condition of product licensing."[22] Otherwise, vaccine manufacturers will continue to ignore such studies, saving themselves time and money, but leading to the inevitable over-vaccination of our pets. As for individual veterinarians, the AAHA recommends:

> ...in each case, to use clinical skill and knowledge, along with client involvement in the decision, to act in what he or she believes to be the best interest of the patient. This would provide flexibility and allow for deviations from labeled recommendations without risk of liability or censure.[23]

While annual revaccination recommendations may be expedient, convenience should never be the foundation for *any* medical intervention. Many veterinarians are distressed over arbitrary annual revaccination schedules and about imposing unnecessary risks through over-vaccination.

Vaccine Ingredients

Vaccines can be dangerous; it makes sense that the risks increase when an animal is over-vaccinated. All vaccines contain antigens (i.e., viruses, bacteria, or toxins secreted by bacteria), relevant to the disease they are meant to prevent. A parvovirus vaccine, for example, will contain parvovirus. Antigens are generally grown and propagated in a feasible culture media, such as bovine fetal serum or upon host tissues derived from certain animals. The antigen is either weakened or killed by the use of heat, serial passages through various cells, or by disinfectants. Vaccine antigens are not supposed to be able to cause disease, but as repeated experience has shown, they can remain virulent in the final preparation. They *are* capable of causing disease both in the vaccinee and in contacts.

One disinfectant that is commonly used to kill vaccine antigens is formaldehyde (formalin). The use of this extremely toxic and carcinogenic chemical has persisted despite *many* historical lessons demonstrating its inadequacy. Simply put, it does not always work. Instead of inactivating the antigens, the formaldehyde may instead harden the outer gelatinous debris of clumped proteins, leaving the antigens inside untouched.[24] When this unnatural chemical amalgam enters the body, enzymes digest the hardened outer portion, freeing the fully virulent particles to enter cells, replicate and cause disease.

Dr. Harash Narang, a clinical virologist, noted another problem associated with formalin-use in vaccines. The "concentration [of formalin] used is so low [that it does] not kill all of the [pathogens, but]...heating the same vaccine preparation would make it completely safe [and]...it would only take minutes."[25] Formalin-inactivated vaccines have *caused* numerous outbreaks of various diseases.[26] In fact, improperly inactivated vaccines have been at the root of a number of the foot-and-mouth disease epidemics in Europe over the past two decades and of the 1969-1972 Venezuelan equine encephalitis pandemic.[27]

Vaccines also contain a variety of chemicals intended to prevent contamination by extraneous microorganisms. They may include antibiotics and other additives such as mercury or phenol. Adjuvants such as aluminum salts or gel may be used to prolong the immune response. Although these substances may appear in vaccines in small quantities, their consequences can be great. They can have significant detrimental effects on immune cells, on the brain and central nervous system, and on organs. For example, one distraught family noted that Kelly, their German shepherd, began experiencing seizures, and Tom, their cat, developed leukemia and died, within four weeks of vaccination.[28] The vaccine antigens and chemicals clearly had adverse effects on these previously healthy animals.

Despite the use of preservatives, vaccines can become contaminated with *undetected* extraneous microorganisms. In 1994, for example, a combination canine vaccine was contaminated with a bluetongue virus which caused abortion in, and subsequently killed, a number of pregnant bitches.[29] Although not scientifically confirmed, this vaccine was also believed to have caused decreased reproduction in some vaccinates and diminished endurance in Alaskan sled dogs.[30] Bluetongue is typically a disease found in sheep and occasionally in cattle. It logically had been assumed that the bovine fetal serum used during production was at fault but a variety of tests performed on the serum were negative for the virus.[31] The definitive source of the contamination was never discovered.

Another concern has recently arisen over the use of bovine fetal serum in vaccine production: the transmission of Bovine Spongiform Encephalopathy (BSE, also known as Mad Cow Disease). BSE causes vacuoles (small spaces) in the brain which gives the appearance of sponginess.[32] Those affected will exhibit trembling and ataxia (physical incoordination). It was believed that BSE was transmitted primarily through the ingestion of infected meat and bone meal, which were frequently fed to cattle and other animals before bans were imposed on the practice.[33] It was asserted, without proper investigation, that calves less than 30 months were safe because signs of the disease were not apparent before that time, so it was also assumed that fetal calf serum was safe. However, recent studies have demonstrated that the disease can be transmitted even if there are no signs, and it can be transmitted in utero.[34] BSE is heat resistant, with boiling having no apparent effect. When the causative agent is heated at 250° Farenheit (121° Celsius) for 15 hours, it still remains at least partially infective.[35] Thus, the use of bovine fetal serum in vaccines provides a potentially significant means of transmission both to animals and humans.

BSE may have emerged in cattle due to a laboratory accident or from a vaccine. Sheep spleens, brains and spinal cords were used to prepare a vaccine against Louping-ill virus in Britain during the 1930s.[36] Sheep vaccinated with this vaccine developed scrapie. BSE appears to have originated from Type II scrapie.[37] Vaccines always carry a risk of contamination from a variety of pathogens that may lurk in the host tissues, media culture, or may be present in the manufacturing laboratory.[38]

Veterinary vaccines, like their human counterparts, require careful consideration. Even if a vaccine is relatively free of extraneous microorganisms, it still contains its own pathogens, plus toxic and carcinogenic chemicals, which can cause devastating and irreversible effects. In many cases, the risks associated with vaccines are simply not warranted because the disease in question may be mild or virtually absent. In other cases, the risk is not warranted because the vaccine is not effective. Each animal should be assessed individually based upon health status, family medical history, environment, stress, and whether the disease in question will pose an actual risk to your pet.

Vaccine Types

The type of vaccine chosen can also affect safety and, in fact, efficacy. There are a number of different types of vaccines currently available. As technology continues to evolve, there will be even more types en route. The most common vaccine types are *modified live* vaccines (MLV) and *inactivated* (killed) vaccines. Although MLVs are less stable than their inactivated counterparts, they are usually more effective because they tend to elicit a stronger, and longer, immune response after fewer doses. They can also be administered earlier than inactivated vaccines.[39] However, live vaccines may cause fetal harm and some have been found to be immunosuppressive, leaving the vaccinee more susceptible to disease for a certain period of time following vaccination. MLVs contain attenuated (weakened, *not* dead) antigens that can replicate in, and be shed by, the vaccinee. Modified live vaccines are more likely to cause vaccine-induced disease, and infect nonimmune contacts, than inactivated vaccines. Viruses found in MLVs can revert back to their virulent forms after replicating in the host. When the animal sheds the virus, "it is...as deadly to other animals as it was prior to vaccination."[40] Even if prelicensure studies demonstrate that the vaccine virus will not revert to virulence, use in the field may yield different results.[41] Prelicensure studies generally use healthy animals. The effect may be different for an animal that is immunocompromised, or receiving simultaneous vaccines, drugs or treatments, has undergone surgery recently, or that may be infected, even if subclinically, at the time of vaccination.

Due to the potential risk of vaccine-induced infection, some vaccines can only be produced in an inactivated form. Inactivated, or killed, vaccines contain antigens that should not reproduce in the vaccinee yet still elicit an immune response. Inactivated vaccines are considered to be more stable and safer than modified live vaccines but they often produce a poor or inadequate immune response. Inactivated products generally contain an adjuvant (antibody booster) to prolong the immune response but adjuvants tend to cause a significant number of adverse, usually inflammatory, reactions. Swelling and nodules at the injection site are common side effects.

Newer vaccine types recently reached the market. *Recombinant* vaccines utilize one type of attenuated antigen to house selected genetic material from another. The combined, genetically engineered hybrid *should* elicit an immune response to both antigens at once, eliminate the need for adjuvants, and contain only nonpathogenic segments of the target antigen. However, this technology is relatively new. Human recombinant vaccines have produced some extremely unfavorable results, such as provoking autoimmune diseases.[42]

Subunit vaccines utilize one component of an antigen, e.g. the outer surface protein, which should elicit an immune response without causing the disease in vaccinees. Subunit vaccines do not generally elicit an effective immune response; many booster doses of vaccine may be required. Also, subunit vaccines frequently require an adjuvant because the immune system may not detect, and therefore not respond to, the altered antigen.

Edible vaccines are currently being developed for a number of diseases. Key genes from the antigens are inserted into edible plants where they can replicate. Edible vaccines can be made cheaply and delivered easily. However, it would be very difficult to prevent overdose, to predict long term effects in vaccinees, to ascertain the potential for antigenic mutation, and to prevent the wholesale contamination of soil, vegetation and ground water that would ultimately occur. Regarding edible veterinary vaccines, it would also be difficult to restrict consumption to the specific animal targeted.

There are significant problems inherent to each vaccine type. Frequently, either safety *or* efficacy is achieved, but not both. There simply is no vaccine that is completely safe and effective regardless of the type used.

Canine

In this chapter, several canine diseases, and the vaccines that have been developed for them, will be thoroughly examined. These include: Parvovirus Type 2, Coronaviris Enteritis, Distemper, Infectious Canine Hepatitis, Kennel Cough, Leptospirosis, Lyme Disease, and Rabies. (A summary of canine vaccine safety and efficacy findings may be found in Table 1 on page 59.)

Parvovirus Type 2

Canine parvovirus infections (and mink enteritis) appear to have descended from a virus that was at one time unique to cats—feline panleukopenia. Many studies have demonstrated a high degree of similarity between the "three" viruses. Although parvoviruses are generally species-specific, something occurred which allowed this "feline" virus to suddenly cross natural species-barriers.

In 1978 and 1979, simultaneous canine parvovirus epidemics, causing fatal myocarditis (heart muscle inflammation) and enteritis (inflammation of the intestines causing diarrhea), occurred in Africa, Australia, Canada, Europe, and the USA.[1] This canine pandemic could not be explained by the virus *naturally* expanding its host range, as some studies suggest.[2] The virus is quite stable in nature. There are a series of genetic changes that would have to occur in order for it to become infective in a previously resistant host.[3]

In fact, many experimental attempts to infect dogs with the naturally-occurring feline panleukopenia virus (FPV) had failed. Canine sera collected before 1976 in Europe, and before 1978 in North America, did not contain any antibodies to the virus.[4] Quite simply, this was an entirely new disease in the dog population. It seems quite likely that the changes required for this feline disease to become virulent in dogs occurred in the laboratory.

It has been suggested that the wild-type FPV was adapted to canine cells either deliberately in the production of attenuated (weakened) live FPV vaccine or accidentally by contamination of canine cells in laboratories. After mutating to dog virulence, the virus could have been spread worldwide with any vaccine produced in canine cells.[5]

Attenuation of the virus by repeated serial passages through canine cell cultures could easily generate the necessary changes. Once this virus is introduced into a new host—in this case, dogs—it will rapidly mutate further. As with any newly introduced disease, consequences will be serious because the new host will not have pre-existing immune defenses capable of addressing the disease.

The canine variant of feline panleukopenia was isolated in 1978 and called *canine parvovirus type 2* (CPV-2).[6] (Interestingly enough, CPV-2 did not appear to be capable of infecting cats, but further mutations, called CPV-2a and CPV-2b, do infect cats. CPV-2b is somewhat more severe than CPV-2a. In North America, it is more common. In Europe, CPV-2a and CPV-2b are equally common.[7]) Infected dogs may remain asymptomatic, or vomit, or have diarrhea for a day. However, a more intense clinical disease may be triggered by stress or exacerbated by concurrent illness or parasites.[8] Furthermore, certain breeds, i.e. Rottweilers, German shepherds, Doberman pinschers and Labrador retrievers, are apparently more affected than others.[9] The disease is most serious in puppies less than eight weeks of age. They can develop myocarditis, an inflammation of the heart's muscular walls. Myocarditis can cause a progressive cardiac insufficiency, cardiopulmonary failure, and death. Myocarditis was more common when CPV-2 first emerged in dogs but has become relatively rare because most bitches will have been exposed, and therefore capable of providing passive immunity to their pups during the vulnerable period. In older dogs that develop signs, the disease takes an enteric (intestinal) form. Signs include vomiting, diarrhea (often containing blood or mucous, particularly with type 2 or type 2a), dehydration, lethargy, anorexia, leukopenia (a reduction of white blood cells), and sometimes fever. Most dogs will recover with proper supportive care: fluids, electrolyte solutions as required, and vitamins. In severe cases, there *may* be a possibility of infertility or birth defects. Some dogs will die within hours of the onset of clinical signs, particularly if the viral load is high and the animal's immune system is otherwise stressed.[10]

Transmission of the virus occurs through contact with infected dogs or feces-contaminated objects. The virus can be shed in feces for approximately three weeks, but shedding may also occur periodically by recovered carriers of the disease. Vomit may also carry the virus, so it is important to disinfect with bleach any area where the dog may have vomited or defecated. It is wise not to introduce a new pet into the household until one month following the recovery, or death, of an infected dog.

A veterinarian should be consulted if vomiting and diarrhea are not resolved within 24 hours or if symptoms become more severe. The dog's magnesium, potassium, and blood sugar levels should be monitored. Some veterinarians will administer pain medication, or specific antibiotics if a secondary bacterial infection is present, but both treatments must be administered cautiously since they have the potential to make the condition worse.[11]

The Canine Parvovirus Vaccine (CPV-2):

Initially, feline panleukopenia and mink enteritis vaccines were used on dogs but they were not very effective.[12] Immunity against clinical disease endured less than six weeks and vaccinated dogs shed the virus after challenge.[13] Subsequently developed inactivated CPV-2 vaccines were slightly more effective but managed to interrupt viral transmission for only a few months.[14] In 1980, the first modified live vaccine became available. CPV-2 vaccines are currently obtainable either on their own (monovalent) or in combination with other canine vaccines, such as coronavirus, distemper, kennel cough (i.e., *bordetella* and *parainfluenza*), and leptospirosis.

Achieving consistent efficacy with current modified live CPV-2 vaccines has been problematic.[15] Within three years of the emergence of this disease in dogs, CPV-2 further mutated into CPV-2a and CPV-2b. Vaccines have been developed for these variants but seem to "have no discernable value over efficacious vaccines prepared from original isolates."[16]

Vaccine efficacy varies considerably depending upon the brand used and when the vaccine is administered. In one study, which compared six combination modified live vaccines, three failed to provide protection against infection or death when pups were challenged orally or intranasally with CPV-2a and CPV-2b.[17] One vaccine appeared to reduce mortality but did not reduce infections, and only two of the vaccines studied were found to be effective at preventing infection and disease. In most cases, two doses were necessary to elicit sufficient antibody production. The authors noted that in both the current and previous studies on CPV-2 vaccines, the vaccine virus is shed, but the authors do not indicate the duration of shedding post-vaccination.[18] It has been noted elsewhere, though, that fecal tests will be positive for CPV-2 from 5-14 days following vaccination.[19] It is of significant concern that the vaccine virus sheds because fecal contact is a common route of transmission.

Modified live vaccines appear to be effective for about five years without revaccination, and are apparently protective against CPV-2, CPV-2a and CPV-2b strains, but none of the vaccines are completely protective in pups while maternal antibodies persist.[20] Maternally-derived antibodies neutralize vaccinations for approximately 14-16 weeks, although pups may become vulnerable to CPV-2 infection 2-5 weeks earlier.[21]

CPV-2 vaccine efficacy problems may also stem from mutations of the vaccine-virus during the attenuation (serial passages) process. These viral mutations predominate in the final formula but they cannot induce immunity.[22] It has also been found that high antibody titers following CPV-2 vaccination does not necessarily indicate immunity.[23] A number of CPV-2 vaccines can cause a strong antibody response in vaccinated dogs but the dogs are still not protected from the disease. One veterinarian reported that after the vaccine was used for a number of years, he began to notice more and more parvovirus cases in vaccinated dogs, "some so soon after the vaccine that it appeared the vaccine was causing the disease, or at least making the dogs more susceptible."[24] The experiences of two Dallas neighbors would appear to concur. One man had recently purchased a puppy. Shortly after vaccination, the puppy died of parvovirus. The neighbor, who had a number of unvaccinated puppies all sharing the same outdoor area as this pup, did not contract the disease. Despite frequent exposures, the unvaccinated puppies remained well while the vaccinated puppy died of parvovirus.

Parvovirus vaccines have been found to cause vomiting and/or local injection site reactions.[25] It has also been suggested that the parvovirus vaccine in dogs (and the feline panleukopenia vaccine in cats) is responsible for the increase (or emergence in the case of cats) of autoimmune cardiomyopathy, and the concurrent rise in inflammatory bowel disease.[26] Parvoviruses suppress the immune system. Injecting the live virus, despite attenuation, can have serious implications for the animal's health and for simultaneous vaccination. Vaccine-induced immunosuppression has been well-documented following various vaccines, and it has been found that if the vaccine recipient is harboring a subclinical infection, or becomes exposed to a pathogen, clinical disease can occur.[27] Similarly, administering additional vaccines may be inadvisable. Numerous studies have demonstrated "an immunomodulating effect between canine parvovirus and canine distemper vaccination." Dogs that received both vaccines together succumbed to vaccine-induced distemper.[28] One wonders, as well, what effect this vaccine-induced immuno-suppression may have on reproduction and fetal injury.[29]

Coronavirus Enteritis

Canine coronavirus enteritis (CCV) causes an intestinal disease that closely resembles, but is milder than, canine parvovirus. Although CCV is found worldwide, the clinical disease is uncommon.[30] In fact, most of the literature alleging coronavirus risks *originates from the vaccine manufacturers*. Yet, the virus is actually so rare that many labs are unable to provide serological testing because they simply cannot obtain samples of the virus.[31]

The incubation period is 1-3 days and the disease is generally self-limiting. Many infected dogs will remain completely healthy. CCV has been found in the feces of both well and diarrheic dogs. Canines living in confined, multiple-dog environments, those who are stressed, or have a concurrent intestinal infection are at greatest risk of developing clinical signs. In dogs that do exhibit signs, lethargy, depression, lack of appetite, moderate to severe yellow-orange-colored diarrhea lasting up to ten days, and sudden vomiting, may be seen.[32] In some cases, there may be mild respiratory signs as well as discharge from the eyes and nose. Puppies generally experience more severe signs than older dogs but mortality is extremely rare and would likely be linked with some other underlying condition. Treatment mainly consists of supportive care. As with any enteric disease, fluids are important to keep up proper hydration.

The Canine Coronavirus Vaccine (CCV):
Many veterinarians were surprised that a coronavirus vaccine was produced. The process is very expensive and time consuming so manufacturers generally try to develop vaccines that they can sell based upon the severity, and existence, of the disease. There was no real need for this vaccine. As one veterinarian stated, "many of my colleagues began referring to the coronavirus vaccine as 'a vaccine looking for a disease.'"[33] The disease is rare and usually very mild. For the majority of the dog population, the vaccine is

completely unnecessary. The disease really only becomes a problem if it happens to spread throughout a closed kennel and results in high treatment costs.[34]

Inactivated CCV vaccines were introduced during the 1980s but they offered very limited protection against the clinical disease.[35] In July 1983, a modified live combination vaccine was licensed but quickly withdrawn from the market because of the serious injuries it caused. Within two months, there were between 900-1,000 reported adverse reactions, with 300 deaths.[36] Over a third of the reactions involved injury to the central nervous system. Some vaccinated dogs died suddenly. Other dogs exhibited a variety of signs including lethargy, respiratory infections, pneumonia, diarrhea, vomiting, convulsions, incoordination, paralysis, encephalitis, meningitis, pancreatitis, severe weight loss despite voracious appetites, growth retardation, infertility, and birth defects.[37] It appears that various components of this combined vaccine were at fault—and even worked synergistically—because canine distemper virus encephalitis, canine coronavirus enteritis, canine parvovirus enteritis, as well as a combination of these diseases, were diagnosed using tissue samples from 32 dogs with vaccine-associated illness.[38] Subsequent testing of the vaccine discounted a reversion to virulence of the vaccine strains. Nevertheless, there is little question that the vaccine is indeed immunosuppressive.

Two new CCV vaccines have been developed recently. One contains modified live CCV combined with canarypox-vectored distemper virus.[39] The other contains a modified live feline enteric coronavirus, which is closely-related to CCV. These products are still relatively new, so information is presently limited to promotional material distributed by the manufacturers.[40] Nonetheless, the actual need for a CCV vaccine has yet to be established. The clinical illness, when it does occur, is generally mild and self-limiting. In contrast, CCV vaccines have caused serious, and sometimes fatal, adverse events. They have typically proven to be more detrimental than the disease itself, and do not provide effective or long-term immunity.

Distemper

Canine distemper (also called Carré's disease or Hardpad disease) is caused by a morbillivirus which is closely related to measles and rinderpest viruses.[41] The disease is present throughout most of the world and can infect a number of other animals, including raccoons, ferrets, and foxes. The virus is transmitted primarily via aerosol droplets (e.g. sneezing) but contaminated objects can also be sources of infection. The virus is fairly unstable outside the host and can be eliminated by most disinfectants. Viral shedding can span several months.

Although the virus is quite prevalent, and most dogs will be exposed to it, few will develop the clinical disease. After a brief (3-6 days) asymptomatic incubation period, the dog may become feverish and generally unwell for a few days. The dog will then appear normal for several days before a second fever arises. With this second fever, dogs often experience lethargy, anorexia, and a clear nasal discharge. As the disease progresses, dogs may develop conjunctivitis, a heavier nasal discharge, diarrhea, and skin eruptions on the abdomen or between the hind legs.[42] Some may experience coughing, difficulty breathing, convulsions or seizures. In more severe cases, the dog may develop hardened footpads, muscle twitching, lack of coordination, paralysis, eye problems, pneumonia, and/or encephalomyelitis (inflammation of the brain and spinal cord).[43] According to a study which examined the mechanisms behind distemper encephalomyelitis, it appears that white blood cells become infected and migrate in an atypical manner to organs and the central nervous system.[44] Some degree of encephalitis (ranging from mild and asymptomatic to profound) may occur in the early stages but only a small number of animals will experience permanent effects.[45] In very young dogs infected prior to the eruption of permanent teeth, teeth may become pitted and discolored.[46]

According to Dr. Richard Pitcairn, certain drugs appear to increase the risk of encephalitis (inflammation of the brain). He recommends homeopathic treatment, fasting (except for vegetable broth and water) during the acute phase of distemper with fever, supplementing the dog with vitamin C to improve immune function, and bathing the dog's eyes for comfort and to aid healing.[47] Canine distemper is immunosuppressive; the strength of the dog's immune system, and the interventions used, will influence the outcome.[48]

The Canine Distemper Vaccine (CDV):
Inactivated canine distemper vaccines have been available since 1923, but they are considered inadequate and have largely been replaced by modified live products. Measles and distemper viruses are so closely related that, in many countries, measles virus vaccines have been used to vaccinate puppies against distemper:

Heterotypic measles virus has been used to surmount maternal antibody interference. Measles virus (MV) is not neutralized by CD virus antibody and behaves like inactivated CD vaccine by provoking limited immunity that protects dogs against illness, but not from infection (Baker, 1970; Slater, 1970; Appel et al, 1984). To achieve optimal immunization of young pups, measles virus has been combined with CD and hepatitis vaccines (Ackermann, 1966; Brown et al, 1972; Burgher et al., 1958; Cabasso et al., 1958; Wilson et al. 1976).[49]

The measles virus is capable of inducing both measles and canine distemper antibodies, with the latter appearing in lower levels.[50] "Dogs inoculated with MV are protected against later challenge with virulent CDV even if measurable CDV antibody is not present."[51] On the other hand, canine distemper virus antibodies do not appear to provide protection against measles.

As a matter of interest, CDV antibodies appear to be "widespread in the U.S. [human] population."[52] In 1962, it was discovered that children develop both measles and distemper antibodies following natural measles infection.[53]

Both antibodies were acquired, with the measles antibody appearing between the 5th and 7th day after onset of illness. In contrast, the distemper-neutralizing antibody appeared later and the titers were lower. The titers of both antibodies persisted for six months with no loss.[54]

In a study comparing the efficacy of measles and canine distemper viruses in beagle puppies, dogs given either vaccine were able to survive challenge with a virulent CDV strain while "control" puppies (which received the parvovirus vaccine) suffered severe clinical signs.[55] Sixty percent of the dogs that received a measles vaccine, and 20% of those receiving the CDV vaccine, developed abdominal petechial rashes, while 20% of the puppies that received the measles vaccine experienced a high fever.[56] The CDV vaccine elicited a rapid antibody response in 78% of the puppies, and although the response was somewhat "sluggish" in the other pups, all vaccinates were protected against challenge.[57]

Overall, current CDV vaccines are considered to be effective but they will be less effective if even low levels of maternal antibodies persist.[58] Still, outbreaks of distemper, including severe clinical disease, have been reported in vaccinated populations.[59] For example, in 1994, Finland experienced a significant outbreak of distemper. Disease incidence was estimated to be in the range of 5,000 infected dogs with a 30% mortality rate.[60] Of 865 confirmed cases, 620 (71.7%) were vaccinated, while 37 (4.3%) were unvaccinated; vaccination status was unknown for 208 (24%) of the dogs.[61]

Duration of immunity varies depending upon the vaccine used and upon the study consulted. Early studies, which were the likely basis for the annual revaccination recommendation, reported a decline in neutralizing antibodies in 33% of vaccinated dogs within one year of vaccination.[62] Such was the case for Sweetie, a German shepherd, who contracted distemper within six months of her vaccination. The vaccine did nothing to prevent infection or the development of the clinical disease. More recent studies indicate that adequate levels of neutralizing antibodies persist for more than six-and-a-half years for some vaccines, and between 3-5 years for others, so annual revaccination is unnecessary.[63]

Modified live canine distemper vaccines have caused a series of problems. Studies have implicated the vaccine in fatalities, encephalitis in immunosuppressed animals, and a potential for the vaccine virus to revert to its virulent form, creating a risk of vaccine-induced disease.[64] Parvovirus-infected dogs will not produce an adequate antibody response to the distemper vaccine and are at increased risk of vaccine-induced encephalomyelitis.[65] Similarly, combining the infectious canine hepatitis vaccine (CAV-1) with the distemper vaccine has been found to increase the incidence of postvaccinal encephalitis in laboratory animals.[66] Vaccines produced using canine cells also have been associated with both postvaccinal encephalitis and the vaccine-virus' reversion to virulence.[67] Further, combining the distemper vaccine with either the CAV-1 or the coronavirus vaccine may enhance virulence of the distemper virus.[68]

Vaccinating pregnant bitches is not advised. It is also important to avoid vaccinating post-whelp until after pups are weaned. Otherwise the pups are placed at risk of vaccine-induced infection. In one study, for example, a healthy bitch whelped ten puppies and three days later received a booster dose of distemper, adenovirus, parvovirus, parainfluenza, and leptospirosis.[69] Although the puppies were previously healthy, 19 days following vaccination of the dam, three puppies began to exhibit neurological signs. In total, five puppies suffered vaccine-induced viral encephalitis and were euthanized. A sixth pup had a transient head-tilt that eventually resolved, but this puppy and another survivor had distemper antibody levels high enough to indicate active distemper infection. The authors suggested that the vaccine virus may have been transmitted through the dam's milk or it may have leaked from the injection site where either the dam or the pups may have licked.[70]

The latter explanation seems implausible. It is doubtful that the dam would have transmitted the virus to her pups by licking the site, then licking the pups, due to the 19-day interval between vaccination and the onset of signs, and due to the unlikelihood of the virus leaking from the injection site.[71] It is even more improbable that five of the 10 pups would have become infected by licking the injection site. The most reasonable explanation is that the vaccine virus was transmitted through the dam's milk.

In humans, it is known that the live attenuated rubella vaccine-virus can be transmitted through breastmilk.[72] Although vaccine manufacturers currently state that it is unknown whether the mumps or measles vaccine viruses can be transmitted via breastmilk, the above study of vaccinated bitches involving the measles-related distemper virus indicates that this issue should be actively addressed. Vaccination in proximity to conception, pregnancy, birth, or while nursing, is not advisable. Dr. F. Edward Yazbak describes this as a period of *immune fragility* and has found that human infants, whose mothers receive the MMR (measles, mumps and rubella) vaccine during this period, are at an increased risk of developing autism.[73]

Over the past few years, Dr. Andrew Wakefield, as well as other well-respected scientists and physicians, have been studying a compelling connection between bowel disease, autism and the measles, mumps and rubella vaccine. It appears that the distemper vaccine is causing the same condition in dogs. Recently, two cases have been presented that show a remarkable similarity to the physiological and behavioral observations made in autistic children. In the first case, Hoss, a Harlequin Great Dane, was vaccinated against distemper and parvovirus at one year of age. Within three months, he began vomiting bile; he had uncontrollable diarrhea and his behavior radically changed. Hoss became obsessive and destructive, even to the point of intense self-injury. He destroys window-coverings and continues to chew his way out of his crate despite severe damage to his mouth. He tends to cower without evident reason. Recently, Hoss was found to be borderline hypothyroid (decreased activity of the thyroid gland).

In the second case, a Yorkie named Kimmer began vomiting bile after her first set of puppy shots. Previously a very calm dog,

Kimmer became obsessive and destructive. She began shredding anything she could, including carpeting, molding and vacuum cleaners, and cannot be kept in a crate because she will destroy her mouth. Her owner recalls Kimmer being completely undaunted by her own "teeth flying" while trying to open her crate. She cannot be distracted, she is very easily frightened, and she literally screams.

In both cases, digestive disorders and behavioral changes, suggestive of autism, have occurred in these dogs following vaccination. Of course, even in autistic children, there is a vast range of behaviors; one will not necessarily see the same conduct in one child as in another. The same would be true of animals. For example, not all children, or animals, will demonstrate self-destructive behaviors. While some may be over-sensitive to sensory stimuli, others may be under-sensitive, and the result could be self-injury.

It is quite interesting that both the measles virus and the distemper virus are of the same genera and that their related vaccines appear to cause the same physiological and behavioral manifestations in children and in dogs. Clearly, these similarities should receive significant scientific investigation.

Infectious Canine Hepatitis

Infectious canine hepatitis (ICH) is caused by canine adenovirus type 1 (CAV-1), found throughout the world. ICH primarily affects dogs and foxes, but not humans.[74] The virus is spread through contact with infected urine. Infected dogs can shed the virus for six months. Although the virus can survive outside of the host for months, it is easily neutralized with a 3% solution of household bleach.

Many infected dogs will have only a subclinical illness. Some may experience a slight fever, perhaps accompanied by congestion or anorexia. In dogs that develop more obvious clinical signs, one might see a fever of over 104°F (40° C), swollen tonsils, coughing, depression, vomiting, anorexia, increased thirst, gastrointestinal disturbances, conjunctivitis, discharge from the eyes and nose, abdominal tenderness, and corneal clouding ("hepatitis blue eye").[75] If the illness is particularly severe, the blood's clotting ability may be compromised. The liver, kidneys, and gallbladder may become inflamed and lesions could develop.

As with other diseases, young puppies are at greater risk of developing complications than older dogs. It is entirely likely that an older dog will develop no remarkable signs. Puppies that do not have sufficient passive immunity may develop chronic hepatitis. Mortality is fairly high in very young puppies and may occur within hours of the onset of signs. Traditional treatments in severely affected dogs may include antibiotic therapy and intravenous dextrose (unless the dog is experiencing prolonged clotting).[76] However, there are a variety of natural therapies available that will help support proper liver function.[77] A holistic veterinarian will be able to prescribe an effective protocol according to your dog's specific requirements.

The Infectious Canine Hepatitis Vaccine (CAV):

Modified live canine adenovirus (CAV-1) vaccines were developed in 1958 but they were largely abandoned due to safety concerns. Although the vaccine was thought to provide immunity against ICH for at least two years after one dose, "the vaccine induced 'blue eyes' in some dogs, was shed in urine, and produced kidney lesions."[78] Inactivated CAV-1 vaccines are available in some areas but these are generally considered to provide only limited protection.[79] CAV-1 vaccines tend to cause a number of adverse reactions, including uveitis (eye inflammation), "white-blue eyes," and enhanced encephalitis caused by distemper vaccines.[80]

During the 1970s, CAV-2 vaccines largely replaced CAV-1 shots. CAV-2, a closely-related adenovirus, is one cause of infectious tracheobronchitis (kennel cough). The viruses are close enough that CAV-2 vaccines provide cross-protection against both CAV-1 and CAV-2 with fewer adverse effects. The CAV-2 live attenuated vaccine does, however, cause "post-vaccinal anterior uveitis." [81]

One Canadian breeder recounted how her prize Airedale show dog, Beauty, developed blue-eye following vaccination. Beauty had been inadvertantly vaccinated twice within a six-month period and became quite ill. She was put on a raw diet, given a liver/kidney cleansing, and started to improve within a month, although the blue-eye remains detectable under a certain light. It appears that Beauty still has some residual immune problems because she has a tendency toward recurrent yeast infections. As Beauty's owner described this, she also recalled vaccine-induced hepatitis in her brother's Labrador retriever puppies. Within two weeks of vaccination, half of the eight-puppy litter died. The puppies were all healthy prior to vaccination.

Although the incidence of postvaccinal blue-eye and distemper encephalitis has been reduced since CAV-2 strains in vaccines replaced CAV-1, clearly these and other adverse effects can still occur.[82] CAV vaccines are typically available only in combination with other canine vaccines. ICH, however, does not appear to be as common an infection as it once was. In fact, Dr. Martin Goldstein, DVM, states: "Infectious canine hepatitis doesn't exist anymore, so why bother to vaccinate for it?"[83]

Kennel Cough
(Bordetella bronchiseptica and Parainfluenza)

Kennel cough and *infectious tracheobronchitis* are general terms used to describe canine respiratory illnesses that can result from a variety of viruses, bacteria, or mycoplasma.[84] The most common causes are Bordetella bronchiseptica, canine adenoviruses types 1 and 2, canine parainfluenza virus, and canine herpesvirus. The common signs are laryngitis, tracheitis (inflammation of the trachea), and bronchitis. Dogs may experience anything from a dry mild cough to a retching cough. Some dogs may experience anorexia but few other signs are associated with most infections. Depending upon the animal's age, stress factors, environmental ventilation, nutrition and health status, there may be additional signs. The emergence of additional signs such as fever, nasal discharge, depression, plus a productive cough, might indicate a complicating systemic, or whole body, infection (e.g. bronchopneumonia or distemper), particularly in puppies.[85] Older, ill dogs may experience chronic bronchitis. Signs begin to appear 5-10 days post-exposure. Although the disease may persist for up to 20 days, the severity of the cough will begin to diminish within the first five days.

Kennel cough is highly contagious and spreads rapidly, particularly in enclosed environments where many dogs are housed. For this reason, hospitalization is not advisable. Treatment largely consists of good general care including proper nutrition and hygiene, and avoiding extreme temperature, ventilation, or humidity variations. Since the disease is ordinarily self-limiting, most dogs will recover very well without further intervention. Extremely ill dogs may be given cough suppressants or antibiotics, but they are rarely indicated. If the infecting pathogen is viral in nature, the use of antibiotics is useless at best and will unnecessarily burden the dog's immune system. The efficacy of antibiotics, even for the bacterial Bordetella bronchiseptica, is quite limited, and may increase the potential for antibiotic-resistance while doing nothing to improve the dog's condition.[86] This appears to be particularly true of systemic treatment because the antibiotic will not even reach the bacteria. Aerosol antibiotic treatment also is of questionable value since it reduces bacterial densities in the trachea and bronchi only temporarily and may cause labored breathing.[87] If an antibiotic is indicated (e.g. for severely ill dogs or those with impaired bronchial-clearing mechanisms), it should be chosen based upon the results of specific culture and sensitivity tests.

The Kennel Cough Vaccine:

The first Bordetella bronchiseptica vaccines were whole cell, inactivated, parenteral (injectable) vaccines. They were not well-accepted by veterinarians due to their high reaction rates. Dogs often experienced swelling and tissue damage at the injection site, and the vaccine was known to cause fatal anaphylactic shock depending upon the concentration of the antigen.[88]

Canine parainfluenza and Bordetella bronchiseptica combined vaccines have been available since the 1970s. They contain either modified live parainfluenza and inactivated B. bronchiseptica antigens for the parenteral vaccine or modified live antigens for the intranasal vaccine.[89] The intranasal vaccine may also contain CAV-2, and is considered to be more protective because it does not appear to be neutralized by maternal antibodies. It is said to protect against both infection and disease, whereas the parenteral vaccine protects only from disease.[90] Dogs vaccinated parenterally are still quite capable of infecting other susceptible dogs. A parenterally vaccinated dog becomes a potential source of infection for every dog he meets, for a period of time, *whether vaccinated or not.*[91] The intranasal vaccine is considered protective after one dose whereas the parenteral vaccine requires two doses and tends to cause local reactions. Differences in efficacy between the two types results from each vaccine's ability, or lack thereof, to elicit necessary mucosal immunity.[92]

One study, designed to demonstrate the safety and efficacy of the intranasal vaccine, presented some interesting results.[93] Thirty dogs were vaccinated against parainfluenza and B. bronchiseptica; ten dogs served as unvaccinated controls. All dogs were then challenged with virulent parainfluenza 18 days later, and with B. bronchiseptica three days after that. None of the vaccinated dogs developed clinical signs (cough) while 9 of 10 controls developed a cough. What is interesting about this study is that investigators tested the dogs for the presence of the virus and the bacteria— through nasopharyngeal swabbing—from the date of vaccination to a few weeks following challenge. Parainfluenza was recovered from vaccinated dogs following vaccination and from unvaccinated controls following challenge. In vaccinated dogs, the virus persisted for an average of 4.87 days while it persisted in controls for an average of 5.1 days. Even more interesting is that the B. bronchiseptica bacteria persisted in vaccinated dogs far longer (27.1 days) than in unvaccinated controls (17.0 days).[94] One cannot help but question the "efficacy" and safety of vaccination over natural exposure. Further, it is known that B. bronchiseptica infection, even if asymptomatic, has a synergistic effect, whereby concurrent infections can be enhanced.[95] There is reason, then, to be concerned if a recently vaccinated dog becomes infected with another organism.

The parenteral vaccine has been associated with anaphylactic (life-threatening allergic) reactions. The intranasal vaccine has been linked with upper respiratory illnesses.[96] Inadvertent injection of the intranasal vaccine is known to cause liver failure. In one case, for example, a fox terrier was injected with the intranasal parainfluenza B. bronchiseptica vaccine and developed a local reaction—necrosis (tissue death)—degeneration of the liver, thrombocytopenia, as well as a variety of other abnormalities.[97]

Typically, Kennel cough presents only a mild, self-limiting disease that is easily manageable with basic supportive care. Since the vaccines have a tendency to cause various reactions, not to mention infection itself, one would be well-advised to weigh whether vaccination provides any real benefit.

Leptospirosis

Leptospirosis is a bacterial disease caused by *Leptospira interrogans,* of which at least 200 serovars (distinct subgroups) exist. Leptospirosis can infect a variety of species, including humans, with varying effects.[98] Infections are most commonly noted in rats. Excluding occasional outbreaks, canine infections are extremely rare. *L. canicola* and *L. ichterohaemorrhagiae* used to be the serovars responsible for most canine infections, but recently there has been a shift to *L. pomona* and *L. grippotyphosa.*[99] In some areas, such as Canada and Long Island, New York, another shift has occurred and different serovar infections have been reported.[100] There does not appear to be significant cross-immunity between serovars so recovery from one type will not preclude infection with another. Simultaneous infections with multiple serovars have been reported.

Infection most commonly occurs during the summer and fall

when environmental conditions, i.e. warmth, moisture and neutral soil pH, are optimal, but they can occur later in the season if there is a mild winter.[101] Infection generally results from direct (skin or mucous membrane) contact with infected urine but it can also occur through contact with contaminated water or food. The incubation period lasts from 4-12 days. Dogs may experience fever, lethargy, pain, vomiting, dehydration, oral ulcers, and pain. Some dogs will suffer an acute form of the disease while others will have either mild symptoms or no signs whatsoever. Clinical manifestations appear to be serovar-dependent.[102] Leptospira shedding can occur for extended periods regardless of whether the dog develops clinical signs.[103] Shedding may take from 4-10 days to begin after clinical signs emerge, and may persist even if antibiotics are administered.[104] In the most serious cases, dogs may experience jaundice, eye inflammation, meningitis, abortion, liver and/or kidney failure. Treatment consists primarily of fluid therapy, supportive care, and antibiotics. Antibiotics are generally administered in two stages: penicillin is given to eliminate the bacteria from the blood, and doxycycline is given to remove the carrier state.[105]

The Leptospirosis Vaccine:

Although there may be *some* resistance to infection between serovars following natural infection, there is no such resistance following vaccination.[106] Vaccines must contain serovars that are prevalent within the particular geographic region to be of any viable benefit. Canine leptospirosis vaccines contain only *L. canicola* and *L. icterohaemorrhagaie* even though there has been a shift to other serovar infections. In other words, for many dogs the vaccine will be utterly useless, addressing serovars that will not pose a threat while neglecting local serovars. In one study, which examined 17 cases, only three dogs were known to be unvaccinated against leptospirosis.[107] One dog had been diagnosed more than three years following vaccination, one within two years, one was vaccinated within one year, while nine dogs had been vaccinated within six months of diagnosis.[108] Vaccination status was unknown for two dogs. The infecting serovars were identified primarily as *pomona* and *grippotyphosa* but there was also evidence of serovar *hardjo* in one dog.[109] Clearly the vaccine does not protect against infection with serovars not included in the vaccine.

The efficacy of leptospirosis vaccines is extremely variable and short-lived. The initial series is comprised of 3-4 inoculations to be followed by annual or semi-annual boosters, depending upon the circumstances.[110] While it appears that the vaccine may prevent clinical disease for up to one year, it does not prevent infection, and appears to prevent shedding for only a few weeks. *If* dogs develop antibody titers following vaccination, they are very low and persist for about 1-3 months.[111] Commercial vaccines generally contain serum proteins from culture media; this increases the potential for anaphylactic reactions.[112] Many veterinarians do not use this vaccine because they tend to encounter few cases of the disease, the duration of immunity is so limited, and because of the unwarranted potential for adverse reactions.[113]

Lyme Disease

Lyme disease is a geographically-restricted illness caused by a bacteria, *Borrelia burgdorferi,* transmitted through the bite of Ixodes (deer) ticks. Typically, the ticks will hatch without sufficient bacteria to induce infection, but as they develop they attach themselves to three different hosts. Their first two hosts are usually white-footed mice, which are frequently infected. As the tick feeds, it ingests the bacteria. It is believed that the bacteria then moves from the tick's gut into its saliva where the tick can transmit the bacteria to a host.[114] The third host is generally a larger animal. While white-tailed deer comprise the most common third host, ticks will attach themselves to dogs, cats, horses, cattle, or humans.[115] Infections are seasonal and correspond to the ticks' feeding cycles (e.g. late spring to fall).

Lyme disease is difficult to diagnose using current serological tests because there are an inordinate number of false-positive and false-negative results. The incubation period may extend over several weeks. Antibodies may persist for a period of months to years, long after the clinical disease resolves, so the presence of antibodies is of questionable diagnostic value.[116] Veterinarians must rely on a combination of criteria in making a diagnosis: exposure to ticks in an endemic area, clinical signs, a positive serology, response to antibiotic treatment, and ruling out other similar diseases.[117]

In endemic areas, approximately 80% of dogs will be seroposi-tive, showing an antibody response to infection with *B. burgdorferi,* but only about 5% will develop clinical signs.[118] Signs include: fever, depression, lethargy, anorexia, swollen lymph nodes, muscle pain, and abnormalities of the joint and musculoskeletal systems.[119] Joints may become painful and acute, recurring arthritis may develop. The sudden onset of lameness is a primary sign, particularly in very young dogs.[120] In severe cases, which are *rare*, neurological changes (e.g. behavioral changes or seizures), kidney lesions, carditis (inflammation of the heart), interference with the electrical impulses that control the activity of the heart muscle, and fatality, are all possible.

Treatment consists of antibiotics, largely because this is the therapy of choice in humans.[121] While antibiotics may be effective for the joint and limb disease, a significant number of affected dogs will experience only a transient or incomplete resolution of signs because the antibiotic will not clear the organism from the dog's system.[122] Concurrent use of nonsteroidal anti-inflammatory drugs may reduce discomfort but they may also mask signs by suppressing the inflammatory response of the immune system making it difficult to determine whether the antibiotics are beneficial.

The Lyme Disease Vaccine:
Lyme vaccines are relatively new on the market and clearly have a long way to go before they become safe. Even then, it would seem prudent to restrict use to high-risk animals residing in endemic regions, that is, *if* vaccines are used at all.[123] The first canine Lyme vaccine became available in 1990. This inactivated, whole cell, bacterin appeared to elicit a strong antibody response in dogs. Nevertheless, the vaccine was hardly useful because while the antibodies effectively neutralized the antigen *in vitro,* "dogs lacked the response to antigens typically seen in nature."[124] Essentially, the vaccine was ineffective outside of the laboratory.

In laboratory experiments using hamsters, the inactivated vaccine was implicated in causing severe destructive autoimmune arthritis when the animals were later exposed to *B. burgdorferi.*[125] This effect was most prevalent with, but not limited to, exposure in the absence of high antibodies.[126] The rodents' immune cells failed to distinguish between self (the body's own cells) and non-self (the antigen), and attacked both, thus creating an autoimmune state.[127] This process, called molecular mimicry, has been known to occur with human Lyme disease vaccines and hepatitis B vaccines.[128]

The vaccine can induce the disease, causing clinical signs that are indistinguishable from natural infection. In a retrospective study of 528 cases submitted for testing, 371 dogs had been vaccinated.[129] Of these, 247 were symptomatic and 53% (131) had antibodies that could be traced back to the vaccine *only*. The vaccine *caused* the disease. In fact, it has been known to produce the disease in dogs residing in areas where the ticks are absent. Dogs that develop the vaccine-induced disease do not generally respond to antibiotic therapy, so treatment strategies are limited to merely masking signs with anti-inflammatory agents.[130] It is also significant that 82 of the 247 symptomatic dogs (33%) had antibodies to both infection and vaccination.[131] In this case, as well as in others noted by the authors, it has been shown that the vaccine sensitizes the animal to natural infection so that exposure *increases* their chance of developing the disease. This is highly significant since only about 5% of naturally exposed seropositive animals would otherwise develop clinical signs.

The vaccine is capable of causing other adverse reactions as well. One owner of a three-year-old Lhasa apso-Shih tzu mix, named McCauley, described another reaction caused by this vaccine. McCauley began having monthly seizures shortly after his 2nd Lyme vaccine. He had received other vaccines previously with no evident reaction but he did suffer from allergies. McCauley experiences both grand mal seizures, involving his whole body, and petit mal seizures, where he will sit motionless and just stare for extended periods of time. Clearly, the Lyme vaccine has the potential to induce a variety of undesirable adverse effects.

Another vaccine, licensed in the U.S. in 1996, appeared promising. This vaccine was directed at eliciting antibodies against a specific *B. burgdorferi* protein, *Osp A,* which was thought to be the first surface protein to which an infected animal would be exposed. After the tick attaches itself, it takes from 24-48 hours for the Borrelia to migrate from its gut to its saliva, where it infects its host.[132] The vaccine should have halted this process because during the 24-48 hour period the tick would be ingesting blood which contains Osp A-specific antibodies. It was later found, however, that when a tick attaches itself to a warm-blooded animal, the antigen stops producing *Osp A* and begins producing a new protein, *Osp C.*[133] Targeting Osp C does not appear to be a solution because studies have shown that Osp C-specific antibodies do not eliminate persistent infection.[134] This vaccine also has been found to induce severe destructive autoimmune arthritis.[135] Vaccines containing a broader array of antigens are currently under development. Lyme vaccines have a very poor track record. Until they are shown to be safe and effective, they are better avoided.

Rabies

Although all warm-blooded animals are susceptible to rabies, it primarily affects carnivores. Different variants of the rabies virus are typically confined to certain geographic locations. For example, one distinct variant will infect dogs and coyotes in Mexico and Texas. A different variant will infect the Arizona fox.[136] Although the different variants are generally identified by their natural reservoir (e.g. "canine rabies" or "skunk rabies"), the variant is not necessarily confined to that species. Cats, for example, are susceptible to all variants even though there is no variant specifically identified as "feline rabies."

Rabies can occur at any time of the year but it strikes more frequently during late summer when wildlife population densities peak. In 1994, the U.S. reported 8,224 cases of rabies in animals, of which only 7% (less than 600 cases) were in domestic animals.[137] The majority of cases result from contact with infected wildlife.[138] Rabies vaccination is often credited with a decrease in rabies cases, particularly amongst dogs, but it is important to note that there are other important factors that have influenced the decrease, including the control of strays, and leash laws.[139]

Rabies is caused by a rhabdovirus. It is transmitted primarily through saliva but can be introduced into fresh wounds by infected tissue fluids or into the mucous membranes through ingestion. Recent studies have suggested that the tonsils are far more important in harboring the virus than the salivary glands.[140] An infected animal can transmit the virus for many days before any clinical signs appear. Animals with inapparent infections can shed the virus for extended periods (months to years) in their saliva.[141] The virus will remain at the site of entry for a considerable length of time, which means that post-exposure treatment can be quite successful. The incubation period can vary considerably: in a dog it may be between 1-18 weeks whereas for horses it can range from 2-9 weeks.

After the virus replicates, it travels through the nerves to the spine and brain, then to the tonsils and salivary glands. Signs of infection vary but may include a change in behavior, loss of appetite, lack of coordination, excessive drooling, aggression, clinginess, convulsions, paralysis and death. Recognizing an infected animal can be tricky, but uncharacteristic actions are reason for caution. For example, nocturnal animals may appear in the daytime. Animals that normally avoid humans will lose their fear and become bold.

In the case of *furious rabies*, aggression is evident. The animal will also be hypersensitive to noise and movement. In cases of *dumb* or *paralytic rabies,* behavioral changes are minimal or nonexistent. The animal will experience paralysis starting in the throat, and will be unable to chew or swallow. While these animals rarely bite, exposure can occur if the owner confuses the condition with choking and examines the animal's mouth bare-handed.[142]

Exposure to rabies does not necessarily guarantee disease or death. Experiments have shown that while some animals will succumb to rabies, others may or may not develop clinical signs and recover completely, depending largely upon the immunocompetence of the host, the infectious dose received, and the site of infection.[143] Other influential factors include the age of the animal and the strain encountered. If the virus has not been completely cleared by the host, reactivation is possible, particularly if the animal becomes stressed and/or immunosuppressed.[144] The frequency with which aborted or inapparent infections occur is unknown because most animals suspected of having rabies are "killed for post-mortem diagnosis; they are rarely given a chance to survive."[145] Rabies may be diagnosed by saliva testing and observation, but it is generally most efficiently diagnosed by examining the brain for the virus.

History of the Rabies Vaccine:

Rabies vaccines have been around since the mid-1880s. Following in the footsteps of Edward Jenner, who developed the smallpox vaccine, Louis Pasteur went on to develop vaccines against fowl cholera, anthrax, rabies, and swine erysipelas.[146] However, Pasteur's seemingly illustrious career was less than ethical because he had a tendency toward denying important contributions of his colleagues. For example, he once used another scientist's vaccine in a public experiment and claimed it was his own.[147] Pasteur's most renowned contribution to vaccine research was his discovery of the rabies vaccine in 1885. Believing that the virus (an unknown entity at that time) was transmitted through saliva, Pasteur injected saliva, taken from the mouth of a rabid dog, into a rabbit's spinal cord. He later harvested and dried the spinal cord to use as a base for his anti-rabies vaccine, which he injected into a healthy animal. This process was repeated hundreds of times until the recipient was able to survive exposure to the original virulent pathogen.[148]

Although the anti-rabies vaccine was intended for animals, Pasteur used it to treat a young boy, Joseph Meister, who had been bitten by a rabid dog. Since it was assumed Meister would die anyway, there seemed to be little harm in administering the vaccine. Pasteur rendered a series of injections over ten days, increasing the strength with each dose. Meister survived. Nonetheless, many of Pasteur's contemporaries claimed that the vaccine was dangerous, taking as many lives as it saved; they declared that many of Pasteur's "cures" were fabricated. When numerous individuals were bitten by the same suspect animal, those who were not vaccinated fared at least as well, if not better, than their vaccinated counterparts. In some cases, the vaccinated person died while the untreated animal remained well.[149] In other cases, Pasteur's miraculously "cured" patients had not been bitten by a rabid animal at all but had only been licked by a perfectly *healthy* one.[150]

Pasteur's rabies vaccine was primarily used in humans. It was not until the 1920s that a vaccine was developed specifically for animals. This vaccine used chloroform or ether to kill the virus. It was prepared from infected brain suspensions.[151] In Asia and Africa, sheep brain cells are still used for both human and animal rabies vaccines and have been suspected in the development of a number of cases of Creutzfeldt-Jacob Disease: the human variant of Mad Cow Disease.[152] A few live attenuated rabies vaccines were developed but they were abandoned because of their ability to cause rabies in vaccinated animals. Current rabies vaccines for domestic animals are inactivated. In recent years, both oral modified live and recombinant rabies vaccines have been used for wild animals.[153]

Canine Rabies

Limiting the dog's contact with wildlife will prevent exposure to rabies in most cases. Leash laws and animal control measures have greatly reduced canine rabies cases. In North America and Europe, about 5% of all reported rabies cases occur in dogs. About 90% of human rabies fatalities have been attributed to rabid dogs.[154] In both the U.S. and Canada, however, human rabies fatalities occur in 0-3 individuals annually. Some cases have actually been caused by corneal transplants harvested from an infected human donor.[155]

Infected dogs may or may not present signs. There have been many reports of unvaccinated and untreated dogs (and other animals) that have had evidence of infection but never developed clinical signs and remained well.[156] Initially, one might note behavioral changes, such as withdrawal or irritation. As the disease progresses, the dog may become aggressive and restless, exhibit a tendency toward snapping or biting, have a high-pitched bark, and trouble swallowing due to spasms and paralysis of the pharyngeal muscle. Drooling may also occur.[157] These signs may be absent or of short duration, in which case the dog may develop paralysis in jaw muscles inducing a dropped jaw and choking sounds. In some cases, an infected dog may simply die without exhibiting signs, or may recover completely.

The Canine Rabies Vaccine:

An interesting phenomena has been observed after rabies vaccination: animals tend to become more aggressive. Although the virus may not be present, the symptoms of the disease will appear either temporarily or permanently. This rabies miasm can appear either after exposure to the pathogen or following vaccination.[158]

> The most common disturbances following rabies vaccination are aggressiveness, suspicion, unfriendly behavior, hysteria, destructiveness (of blankets, towels), fear of being alone and howling or barking at imaginary objects.[159]

Jet, a four-year-old Labrador retriever, displayed signs of rabies miasm following his vaccination. It is possible that his initial puppy shots sensitized his immune system for a much stronger reaction later on. Furthermore, his immunity was low when he received the rabies vaccination. He suffered severe chronic diarrhea for three months prior to the shot and had received antibiotics and deworming medication at that time. Within six weeks he demonstrated clear signs of rabies miasm. He became very frightened, extremely sensitive to touch, jumpy, unfriendly, confused, and he was hallucinating. These episodes were initially frequent but were spaced further apart over the next four months until they dissipated.

In another instance, Sport, a Retriever-mix who had previously been quite gentle and submissive, became aggressive following a rabies vaccine received at 7½ years of age. Although the aggression has diminished, she developed a fear of her food bowl. Sport also exhibited a number of reactions that have been reported by many other pet owners following vaccination: an extended period of lethargy; the development of allergies, skin and coat problems, and an increase in, and allergy to, fleas.

Although adverse effects can arise when only one vaccine is given, they appear more frequently when several vaccines are given simultaneously. Therefore, it is wise to administer the rabies vaccine separately, with a 4-6 week interval between administering others.[160] Dr. Pitcairn reports that homeopathic treatment for vaccine-induced miasm has been effective, albeit difficult at times. The animal will experience a relapse, or another reaction, when revaccinated.[161]

Such was the case for Remington Steele, a two-year-old Blue Dane. He developed a tremor in his left leg after his first rabies vaccine at six months of age. Since his veterinarian did not recognize this as a vaccine-reaction, the dog was revaccinated one year later. Shortly thereafter, a tremor developed in the right leg, where he had been vaccinated. Within three months, Remington Steele was lame in both legs. He became depressed, lethargic, lost his appetite, and experienced grotesque swellings throughout his body. His condition soon became critical as he began bleeding "out of every vein," as well as from his nose and eyes. He remained in the hospital for one week and returned home 19 pounds thinner—with no adequate diagnosis to explain his condition. He is now being treated homeopathically and his condition is improving.

Vaccine-induced rabies is also a significant concern. For example, three dogs became infected with rabies 12-14 days after vaccination with a modified live Flury-strain vaccine.[162] Paralysis began in the vaccinated hind limbs, spread to the other hind limbs, then affected the forelimbs to some degree. It is believed that the vaccine virus reached the spinal cord by traveling along the sciatic nerve but "stopped short of causing complete quadriplegia in two of the cases."[163] High levels of rabies antibodies were found in the cerebrospinal fluid of the dogs, exceeding even the levels in the serum. This reaction was previously unseen in dogs but had been noted in humans with prolonged survival or recovery from natural rabies infections. There was no evidence of the rabies virus in the dogs' saliva. In the first two cases, the dogs survived and paralysis resolved within a few months. The third dog, which was believed to have had a concurrent naturally-acquired distemper infection, died. The study noted that the rabies virus "contributed to the disease syndrome in the third dog."[164]

In one household, two dogs experienced serious adverse reactions to the rabies vaccine. Both dogs exhibited lameness but the course of the vaccine-induced illness differed for each animal. Yogi, a 12-year-old male Lab-Boxer mix, and Polly, an 11-year-old Lab-Retriever mix, both received their rabies vaccine on the same day in late 1999. Yogi developed a large lump at the vaccination site and was lame for four days. A week later, he had an open abscess around his right eye. Over the next two weeks, he lost all of the skin (not just the fur) on the right side of his face and then on his right thigh. His gums weakened so that he could not eat. His owner recalls that he rapidly lost 30 pounds, limped, and "lurched like a rabid dog with foam dribbling from his mouth." He lost bladder control, his kidneys failed, and he became paralyzed. Yogi was then euthanized. Polly seemed to remain healthy for 1½ years after the vaccine, but in July 2001 she began sneezing blood and developed occasional lameness in her hind right leg where she had been vaccinated. A walnut-sized tumor developed on her snout which, by the following February, covered the entire right side of her face. At that point, the lameness returned and remained. For the second time in two years, the owners had to euthanize their pet because of rabies vaccine-induced disease.

Focal necrotizing granulomatous panniculitis (a chronic inflammation of fat beneath the skin with hardened skin and tissue death) has resulted from rabies vaccination. Over a period of two years, 13 dogs with such lesions were observed at the Ontario Veterinary College.[165] Ten of the dogs were Poodles, two were Bichon frises, and one was a Shih tzu. Most lesions were discovered after clipping/ grooming sessions. Although there appears to be a breed predilection associated with this reaction, it may well be that the reaction was observed more often in poodles due to the frequency with which they are groomed and the type of clipping they receive.[166] Lesions were characterized by hardened skin, fat necrosis, inflamed blood vessels, decreased blood supply to the area, and alopecia (balding). The lesions were discovered 3-6 months following administration of different rabies vaccines. One dog developed the same response in three different sites following three annual rabies shots, using two different vaccines. Another dog died from anaphylaxis when revaccinated. Barring the anaphylaxis, the authors theorized that inadvertent subcutaneous, versus muscle, administration of the vaccines may have led to the reactions. However, one must ask, if we are seeing this sort of reaction when the vaccine is administered closer to the skin's surface, what must be happening at the deeper levels when the vaccine is administered properly?

The rabies vaccine can cause a large number of adverse reactions. Seizures may develop or be exacerbated by the vaccine. Many animals develop tumors, become aggressive, or suddenly start wasting away. Gunny, an Epi Beagle, began having seizures at 14 years of age. Although his condition had stabilized, the seizures began to recur following rabies vaccination, and progressed to cluster-seizures within three days. Similarly, Precious, a Lab mix, began having seizures following her vaccination at ten years of age. They seemed to be under control until she was given her next rabies vaccine and the cycle started all over again.

Harley, a five-year-old Standard poodle, had received typical vaccines for the first two years of life, with rabies vaccine given at separate appointments. Following this, he was given only the rabies vaccine. One week after Harley's last rabies vaccination, his temperature soared, his muzzle and abdomen were covered in hives, his testicles became grossly enlarged, he began vomiting, had bloody diarrhea, started seizuring, and developed polyarthritis. After $4000 and six weeks in treatment, no explanation other than a vaccine reaction could be found. After considerable research, Harley's veterinarian will never vaccinate him again.

Groucho, an 11-year-old Border-Collie mix, exhibited a low-grade fever and difficulty breathing for about 24 hours following his distemper and rabies vaccination at eight years of age. His veterinarian did not think this was a vaccine reaction, but a mere coincidence, and suggested seeing what happened after the next year's vaccination. Within two hours of his next vaccination, Groucho's temperature spiked, his breathing was reduced to extremely labored gasps, he stopped eating and drinking, and he had no use of the leg where he received the vaccines. Again, the veterinarian stated that this reaction was a mere coincidence and suggested further vaccination. Although these signs resolved within three days, Groucho has been left with two significant lumps on the leg where he was vaccinated. One lump is the size of a marble; the other is the size of a golf ball. Following vaccination, he also developed skin problems, such as a flaky and itchy rash, and numerous large moles. His owner noted that new growths have declined since they stopped vaccinating Groucho.

Baron, a 12-year-old Kuvasz, began reacting to his second set of annual vaccinations in 1990. He developed a rash on his abdomen and was treated with prednisone. His veterinarian said that this was normal. In 1994, four months after vaccination, Baron developed cutaneous histocytosis, small benign tumors that appear above the skin surface. Baron's condition is exacerbated by stress. Prednisone was prescribed to control the tumors, but as soon as he stopped receiving the drug the tumors would reappear. His owner notes that shortly after vaccination Baron became aggressive towards other dogs and then later towards humans, a condition that has persisted long after vaccination was halted. Since 1996, Baron has received homeopathic remedies and no vaccines or Prednisone. The tumors continue to appear and disappear depending upon his level of stress.

These are just a few examples of the varied adverse reactions dogs may experience following rabies vaccination. Unfortunately, the reactions are not always recognized as being vaccine-related and the animals continue to receive annual or triennial boosters, increasing their chances of having a longer and stronger reaction. Many veterinarians and dog owners feel that they have no alternatives since rabies vaccination is required by law in many—but not all—localities. (In fact, rabies stands in a class by itself in terms of veterinary vaccine mandates because *the rabies vaccine is the only one required by law for your dog.*) Thus, veterinarians and dog owners may be inclined to ignore prior reactions and continue to endanger the animal through further vaccination.

However, as with any vaccine mandate *there are legal provisions—perhaps even exemptions—available when the vaccinee has had a prior reaction, or is experiencing any condition, which would contraindicate further vaccination.* There may also be provisions to avoid vaccinating animals demonstrating sufficient antibody titers. Veterinarians should be aware of provisions and exemptions within their region *and* have this information readily available to all of their clients. If this information is not readily available, clients must then take the initiative and contact their local health departments. It should also be noted that vaccines are intended *only* for *healthy* animals. Any animal that is ill, immunosuppressed, or otherwise stressed, not only has an increased risk of an adverse reaction but also cannot be expected to elicit a sufficient immune response to the vaccine. Vaccinating such animals is not only dangerous, it will be virtually useless, unjustified, and represents malpractice.

While it is unlikely that canine rabies vaccination requirements will be discontinued, it is not unreasonable to demand that laws be re-evaluated. Currently, dogs must be vaccinated every 1-3 years, depending upon the vaccine chosen and local requirements, but there is little evidence supporting such frequent revaccination. In some areas, Texas for example, dogs are required to receive the 3-year vaccine annually "to protect public health by ensuring that the vaccine duration of immunity would still be effective even if owners were tardy in having their pets inoculated."[167] Over-vaccination, with its inherent potential for adverse effects, seems assured. Clearly, the vaccine can cause rabies miasm (chronic disease), all of the clinical signs of rabies, tumors, and a wide variety of other serious reactions. The risk-benefit ratio, and the frequency with which we are administering the rabies vaccine, must be reassessed.

The duration of immunity elicited by rabies vaccines has been poorly researched even though this is perhaps one of the best-studied veterinary vaccines on the market. Studies typically focus upon the *minimum* period during which immunity is expected to endure. The animals are then usually killed after the prescribed study-period. Instead, duration of immunity studies should focus upon the *maximum* length of time that the vaccine can be considered protective. One veterinarian maintains that "one or two doses of rabies vaccine provide...lifetime protection." Indeed, according to a nationwide U.S. study, only one dog and two cats that had received only one dose of the vaccine contracted rabies. There were no cases in any that had received two vaccinations.[168]

Proper 'duration of immunity' studies are imperative to avoid the unnecessary adverse effects associated with over-vaccination and the needless expense this creates for pet owners. Legislation requiring booster doses every 1-3 years should be questioned, and changed, because there is no scientific basis to support repeatedly exposing animals to this vaccine. In some cases, there simply is no epidemiological support for vaccinating certain species (e.g. ferrets and indoor cats). Where rabies vaccine mandates exist, legislators should draft clear provisions to avoid vaccinating any animal that may be at high risk for a reaction, and compensate pet owners for all adverse events and deaths associated with rabies vaccination.

Polyvalent Vaccines

Since most vaccines are administered in combination, it is often difficult to isolate the specific part of the vaccine causing an adverse event. In some cases, a single component may be largely responsible for particular effects. In other cases, it may be a combination of ingredients working synergistically that produce the adverse event.

Combined canine vaccines have been associated with the development of immune-mediated hemolytic anemia (IMHA) in dogs.[169] IMHA refers to a chronic destruction of oxygen-carrying red blood cells. The immune system creates self-attacking antibodies.

It is unknown whether this occurs because the vaccine itself initiates the development of autoantibodies or whether the vaccine is triggering (accelerating) a pre-existing condition that otherwise might not have manifested so soon.[170] Dogs experience a severe reduction in platelets (required for clotting) and an increase in bilirubin (bile pigment in the blood) leading to jaundice, anorexia, and malaise.

While IMHA is known to occur with various drugs, once the medication is withdrawn, the prognosis is generally good. However, one cannot withdraw vaccines, so a poorer prognosis can be expected for vaccine-induced IMHA. Dr. Jean Dodds has been studying IMHA in hundreds of dogs for over two decades and has found that certain breeds appear to be more predisposed to this condition. Furthermore, there is mounting evidence that vaccines trigger IMHA and other autoimmune diseases in genetically susceptible animals.[171]

> Among the more commonly predisposed breeds were the Akita, American cocker spaniel, German shepherd, golden retriever, Irish setter, Kerry blue terrier, miniature and standard dachshund, toy, miniature, and standard poodle, old English sheepdog, Scottish terrier, Shetland sheepdog, shih tzu, vizsla, and Weimaraner.[172]

In another study, which examined the records of 58 dogs listed to have IMHA, a significant number (26%) developed the condition within one month of vaccination (mean time between vaccination and onset of signs was 13 days; range 1-27 days).[173] Sixty percent died and a full 3/4 of those died within three weeks of diagnosis.[174]

One Airedale breeder reported a variety of serious problems after her dogs were given polyvalent vaccines. Her first observation came with Blake, who would become quite ill three weeks after his annual vaccinations. Blake also became extremely phobic so that he would "nearly tear the house down" during thunderstorms. The vaccine reactions became far more pronounced, though, when a number of her bitches and litters became ill. Aster, a five-year-old bitch, whelped a litter of nine puppies. After their second round of vaccines, the puppies became ill. Half of the litter died before the age of three, primarily due to kidney problems. One pup developed hemolytic anemia and one developed thrombocytopenic purpura, both autoimmune blood disorders. One female from this litter lived until about seven years of age, and two males are still alive at age ten. Aster herself developed autoimmune problems at age seven when she was diagnosed with hemolytic anemia. She was being treated with Prednisone. Although this contraindicated further vaccination, her veterinarian continued to vaccinate her. Eighteen months later, she developed thrombocytopenic purpura. At age 12, Aster had another serious bout with hemolytic anemia, also developed lymphoma, and was euthanized.

Misty, a bitch unrelated to Aster, also whelped nine puppies. They reacted to their third round of vaccines and displayed varying degrees of liver damage. One puppy had to be euthanized at six months due to severe liver shunts (underdeveloped vessels). The other pups were given milk thistle and improved. Since this breeder stopped vaccinating her animals, none have demonstrated liver, kidney, or autoimmune problems, and none have died prematurely.

Another dog owner reported the continual decline of her seven-year-old Golden retriever, Holly, following vaccinations. A few years ago, she began having infrequent seizures. Within a few weeks of her last vaccination, administered in November 2001, she stopped eating and drinking and became very weak. A myriad of tests revealed nothing. By February, Holly's weight had decreased from 92 pounds to 58 pounds. Her veterinarian recommended euthanizing Holly but one last attempt was made to improve her condition. She was given Prednisone which increased her desire to eat. Holly's weight climbed to 84 pounds but has again started to decline. In May 2002, Holly was diagnosed with an advanced lymphoma, and was euthanized.

Polyvalent vaccines have the ability to cause many serious adverse events. The number of pathogens plus toxic and carcinogenic chemicals that the animals are exposed to all at once generate an enormous toll on the immune system. The results can be devastating. Vaccines are generally provided in polyvalent forms to reduce the number of injections required, and to assure that vaccines won't be missed because the client fails to return for recall notices. Polyvalent inoculations were not designed to improve the patient's health. *Combined vaccines are merely a convenience.*

TABLE 1:
CANINE VACCINES

Vaccine	Comments
Parvovirus Type 2	Vaccine virus sheds. Efficacy varies. Immunity persists for five years. Local, systemic and autoimmune reactions. Post-vaccination vomiting and diarrhea are common. The vaccine is immunosuppressive and may cause inflammatory bowel disease or autoimmune cardiomyopathy. Administration with CDV vaccine may induce distemper.
Coronavirus Enteritis	Disease is rare, mild, and self-limiting. Earlier vaccines were ineffective or extremely dangerous. Newer vaccines cannot yet be accurately assessed. The nature of the disease does not warrant vaccination.
Distemper	Vaccine efficacy is variable. When effective, immunity may endure 3-5 years. Avoid vaccination in conjunction with parvovirus infection, or with parvovirus or coronavirus vaccines. Vaccine-induced infection, rash, encephalitis, and encephalomyelitis may occur following vaccination. Vaccine virus sheds in milk.
Infectious Canine Hepatitis	Infectious canine hepatitis is a rare disease. Vaccine can cause 'blue eye' and, if administered with the distemper vaccine, encephalitis.
Kennel Cough B. Bronchiseptica and Parainfluenza	A mild disease. Viral shedding occurs longer for infected vaccinated dogs than unvaccinated dogs. Vaccines can cause respiratory illness and anaphylactic reactions. Local reactions accompany parenteral (injectable) vaccines. Inadvertent injection of intranasal vaccine can result in liver failure and tissue death.
Leptospirosis	Variable, serovar-specific, short-duration immunity. Will not prevent infection or shedding. Risk of anaphylaxis.
Lyme Disease	Vaccine induces lyme disease, autoimmune arthritis, seizures, and increases susceptibility to the natural disease. Renders antibiotic treatment useless.
Rabies	Vaccine can induce the disease as well as rabies miasm, tumors, lesions, paralysis, lameness, severe diarrhea, alopecia, skin problems, wasting, allergies, seizures, polyarthritis, etc. Annual and triennial mandates are not supported by science.

Feline

In this chapter, several feline diseases, and the vaccines that have been developed for them, will be thoroughly examined. These include: Feline Leukemia, Feline Immunodeficiency Virus, Infectious Peritonitis, Calicivirus and Rhinotracheitis, Bordetella, Chlamydiosis, Panleukopenia, and Rabies. Ringworm and Vaccine-Induced Sarcomas are also discussed. (A summary of feline vaccine safety and efficacy findings may be found in Table 2 on page 82.)

Feline Leukemia

Feline leukemia virus infection (FeLV) is caused by a retrovirus[1] that can cause immunosuppression, malignancies, severe anemia and reproductive failure.[2] Many infected cats (greater than 70%) will have subclinical infections, or will manifest viral matter in the blood (viremia) yet defeat the virus, inducing immunity. Some infected cats (less than 30%) will develop chronic viremia and further illness.[3] Persistently viremic cats will usually survive for a period of months to years. Cytoproliferative (cell multiplication) and suppressive changes may occur, but one will eventually dominate, leading either to malignancies or immunosuppression and an increased susceptibility to disease over time.[4]

Carriers can shed the virus for 1-16 weeks via nasal secretions, saliva, and urine, underscoring the importance of separating infected cats and utilizing separate bowls, utensils and litter boxes.[5] The virus survives on surfaces up to two hours. The virus can also be transmitted through contact with blood, from a pregnant queen to her kittens, and through her milk.[6] While the virus has been isolated in semen and vaginal fluids, transmission via saliva poses a greater risk than venereal transmission.[7]

Kittens less than four months of age are the most susceptible to infection. Cats four months and older are relatively resistant to the disease. Illness generally requires prolonged intimate contact with an infected cat. Virtually all neonatal kittens exposed to the virus will become viremic versus 70%-85% of weanling kittens. Only about 15%-30% of cats greater than four months exposed to the virus will develop persistent viremia.[8] Depending upon the strain, however, these figures may be greatly reduced. For example, very few, if any, weanlings or older cats will become viremic from the type C strain.[9] The cat's immune status is very important to the outcome, particularly in the first 4-6 weeks after exposure, so proper nutrition, hygiene, and stress factors must be considered.

There is no reliable conventional cure for FeLV. AZT, the same drug used to treat HIV-positive humans, has successfully prevented chronic viremia in cats, but it is of no value once the condition becomes persistent. Often, FeLV is not diagnosed until after the cat has become chronically viremic, when it is extremely difficult to reverse. *Low dose* leukocyte-derived human interferon-*a* has apparently increased survival time but it does not prevent the blood infection. Viremia has been reversed in a few cats through the administration of Staphycoccal protein A (a bacterial cell wall). Perhaps the best treatments are based upon common sense, incorporating those factors that will improve immune functioning, such as good nutrition, hygiene (disinfection of dishes, litter boxes and bedding), stress reduction, and keeping the cat indoors to prevent exposure to other pathogens (as well as preventing transmission to other cats).

The Feline Leukemia Vaccine (FeLV):

The first commercial inactivated feline leukemia virus vaccine promised to reduce the likelihood of persistent viremia, to provide maximal antibody response after two doses and, with a third dose, would assure an even longer period of protection.[10] Upon studying this vaccine, however, Drs. Neils Pederson and Richard Ott found that the company's claims were far more impressive than their supporting data.[11] In a field study, using a prototype of the vaccine, almost 27% of vaccinated cats became persistently viremic within one year. While this was interpreted to mean a 73% vaccine efficacy rate, the result was hardly impressive since the recovery rate for exposed unvaccinated cats is approximately 73%.

Pederson and Ott's independent study found that the antibody responses induced by the vaccine were weak at best. An envelope protein, FeLV-gp70, is considered to be the most important aspect of the virus in creating an immune response.[12] An adequate antibody response to FeLV-gp70 arose in only 13% of cats given two doses of the vaccine and in only 50% of cats given three doses.[13] Cats in both vaccinated and unvaccinated groups developed persistent and active infections almost equally, and both groups experienced exactly the same number of latent infections. It is important to note that there have been reports associating latent infections with the development of FeLV-negative lymphosarcomas, and that "latent infections in queens can also lead at times to active or latent infections in their kittens."[14] Further, it remains possible that latent infections can be reactivated under certain conditions (e.g. when the animal is stressed).

Administering a third dose of the vaccine offered only a slight protective advantage; efficacy was determined to be a mere 25%. Antibodies capable of neutralizing the virus were notably absent in vaccinated cats until they were exposed to the virulent virus. Another claim that was made by the manufacturer, and invalidated by this study, was that the FeLV vaccine afforded protection from other conditions, including "lymphosarcomas, upper respiratory disease and FeLV-associated diseases such as Feline Infectious Peritonitis (FIP)..."[15] The rationale behind this claim was that by preventing the highly immunosuppressive FeLV infections, the vaccine would also reduce incidence of these other conditions. Since the vaccine was found to be ineffective, however, this claim was misleading.[16]

Since the vaccine required a three-dose regimen to produce even mildly favorable results, the company introduced Leukocell-2. With a higher concentration of antigen, it was hoped that the vaccine would induce a better immune response after two doses. In one experiment describing vaccine efficacy, 28% of vaccinated cats became persistently viremic after challenge-exposure.[17] This represents a mere 3% improvement in efficacy over its predecessor.

In a study conducted to compare the efficacy of two inactivated vaccines (Leucat and Leukocell-2) and one subunit-recombinant vaccine[18] (Leucogen), it was found that neither inactivated vaccine provided protection when cats were challenged intraperitoneally (in the abdomen) with the virus.[19] All of the Leucat vaccinated cats became viremic; none produced virus-neutralizing antibodies. Ten of twelve (83.3%) Leucocell-2 vaccinated cats became viremic; only the two (16.7%) that resisted challenge developed neutralizing antibodies. Leukogen vaccinated cats fared somewhat better in that 5 of 12 (41.7%) became persistently viremic while seven (58.3%)

resisted challenge and developed neutralizing antibodies.

The second half of this trial tested the efficacy of Leukogen against exposure to three FeLV subtypes.[20] Only six vaccinated and six unvaccinated cats (controls) were included in the study. Such a small study necessarily precludes any definitive conclusions. However, of the six vaccinated cats, one became persistently viremic three weeks after oronasal challenge with the virus and died. The other five vaccinated cats did not become viremic but only two produced virus-neutralizing antibodies. Of the unvaccinated cats, none died, 5 of 6 became persistently viremic, and none produced virus-neutralizing antibodies. The value of virus-neutralizing antibodies against FeLV is unknown. Thus, efforts should focus on determining whether it is in fact antibodies or other immune mechanisms that elicit an adequate immune response.

In a recent report issued by the American Association of Feline Practitioners (AAFP), the continued discrepancy between vaccine efficacy studies is acknowledged.[21] They state that,

> Because protection is not induced in all vaccinates, preventing exposure to infected cats remains the single best way to prevent FeLV infection.[22]

They also recommend that vaccination against FeLV be limited to those cats at greatest risk of exposure, particularly if less than four months of age, when they are most vulnerable to infection. Cats at risk include outdoor cats, those living with FeLV-infected (or unknown FeLV-status) cats, and those living in multiple-cat environments. *"Vaccination is not recommended for cats with minimal to no risk of exposure, especially those older than four months of age."*[23]

The variable efficacy associated with this vaccine is not the only factor that must be considered. Vaccine-induced infection is a possibility, as one breeder of Persians found. This breeder had never had any cats test positive for the disease but one of her kittens, which was taken to the veterinarian for vaccination against FeLV upon adoption, became ill with the disease almost immediately. The kitten was not in contact with any other cat. The breeder who disclosed this incident noted that she will no longer offer any guarantee on kittens vaccinated against FeLV or, she added, against FIP (infectious peritonitis) which has "a bad reputation among breeders."

The FeLV vaccine has also been shown, along with the rabies

vaccine, to cause more cases of vaccine-induced fibrosarcomas (soft-tissue tumors) than other feline vaccines.[24] The fibrosarcomas tend to be fairly aggressive and recur despite removal and treatment. For example, Shorti, a 12-year-old black and white domestic cat, developed a small tumor on her shoulder after receiving her FeLV vaccine the previous month. Her veterinarian recommended waiting to see what happened. Within six months the lump had increased significantly. Removal meant that Shorti also lost a good deal of muscle and some bone. Within a month of surgery, the lump returned, and a few months later it had grown to the size of a small melon, exceeding the boundaries of her skin and fur. Over the next few months, many attempts were made to help Shorti, but her failing health made it necessary for her owners to end her suffering.

Bean, a nine-year-old domestic short hair, developed cancer following annual vaccinations which included FeLV (rabies was administered triennially). Bean endured nine surgeries to remove the recurring injection-site tumors, as well as chemotherapy, which was followed by renal failure, secondary parathyroid disease and hypertension, resulting in Bean's death.

Vaccine-induced fibrosarcomas are all too common following FeLV vaccination. A previously well cat may suddenly develop an aggressive tumor that recurs despite surgery. For most cats, the risks associated with this vaccine greatly exceed any proposed benefit.

Feline Immunodeficiency Virus

Feline immunodeficiency virus (FIV), also called feline AIDS, is a retroviral (lentivirus) infection that is clinically indistinguishable from FeLV. It shares many similar features with both simian immunodeficiency virus (SIV) and human immunodeficiency virus (HIV). Initially, cats will experience fever, lymphadenopathy (a disorder of the lymph nodes) and neutropenia (a diminished number of neutrophils in the blood).[25] Cats generally recover from this stage. It may be many months or years before the subsequent immuno-deficiency stage begins. When this occurs, cats may experience fever, lymphadenopathy, lethargy, anemia, weight loss, and behavioral changes.[26] As the disease progresses, cats become prone to opportunistic secondary infections of the gastrointestinal, respiratory, and urinary tracts, and of the skin.[27] They are at increased risk of bacterial and fungal infections, kidney dysfunction, and cancer. Some experience neurological signs such as dementia, convulsions and psychomotor disturbances.[28] Infection will persist throughout the cat's life but there is currently insufficient information indicating how many cats will enter the terminal stage of the illness.[29]

In an interesting model of FIV transmission within colonies of free-roaming cats, it has been suggested that FIV has little impact on the total population. A low rate of transmission, the long asymptomatic stage of infection, and the high death rate from other causes combine to minimize the effect of the virus on these cats.[30]

The virus is found throughout the world but incidence is low. For example, in the United States, "overall prevalence of 2% to 4% are usually reported" and some cats have been found to resist infection altogether.[31] The virus is shed through the saliva; biting is the primary mode of transmission. Sexual transmission is unusual. Some FIV strains can be transmitted from an infected queen to her fetuses or nurslings but this is very rare and dependent upon the timing of infection and onset of immunodeficiency.[32] Male cats appear to become infected more frequently than female cats, and outdoor cats are at greatest risk. Incidence is highest amongst sexually intact males due to fighting and biting behaviors. The disease is more prevalent in households where more than six cats reside. The disease is generally discovered in older cats but this is probably due to recognition of the disease after an extended latency period rather than any age-related susceptibility. Fewer cases are found in purebred cats but this likely reflects a difference in lifestyle since purebreds tend to be kept indoors more than mixed breeds.[33]

Conventional treatment generally consists of AZT therapy. AZT tends to have a positive effect on neurologic disease and overall condition but it may cause anemia. Continued use may also lead to the creation of AZT-resistant strains. Immunomodulating drugs that promise to restore the immune system have been tried. Thus far the results have been disappointing.[34] As with many other feline diseases, keeping cats indoors is the best prevention. Spaying and neutering outdoor cats will also reduce fighting and biting behaviors.

The Feline Immunodeficiency Virus Vaccine (FIV):
FIV vaccine development has been fraught with the same overwhelming obstacles confounding HIV vaccine research. FIV, like HIV, mutates rapidly. Even if a vaccine is found to be effective

against the original virus, it is often completely ineffective against mutations or subtypes.[35] There are also questions remaining over which elements of the immune system vaccines should stimulate in order to elicit protection, and which virus components should be included in the vaccine.

In one study, testing three different FIV vaccines, it was found that seven of nine unvaccinated control cats resisted infection while all 13 vaccinated cats became infected with FIV after challenge.[36] Furthermore, the vaccinated cats became viremic sooner than the unvaccinated cats. Candidate FIV subunit vaccines have produced similar results. While many of the vaccinated test cats developed significant virus-neutralizing antibody titers, all became infected with FIV within four weeks of viral challenge.[37] The researchers noted that in this study, and in previous studies with FIV subunit vaccines, "the induction of [virus- neutralizing] antibodies...predisposed for accelerated viremia rather than for protection upon FIV challenge."[38] The vaccine *enhanced* viral replication.

In a study involving an inactivated FIV-infected cell vaccine, vaccinated cats became viremic two weeks following challenge whereas control cats did not become viremic until four weeks post-challenge.[39] The viremia was not only accelerated but was also increased, showing a higher degree of infected cells for the vaccinated cats.[40] Attempts have even been made to induce immunity by combining vaccine types, first using a live viral vector vaccine to prime the immune system, followed by two doses of inactivated FIV-infected cell vaccine. No protection whatsoever was afforded to vaccinated cats.[41] Even the most promising FIV vaccines, at best, can make tentative claims of reducing viremia levels if the cat is infected intravaginally (which is not a significant risk), but they cannot reduce viremia levels following intravenous challenge nor prevent infection.[42] Clearly, the complications facing FIV vaccine researchers are as vexing as those facing HIV vaccine researchers. Both vaccines should be met with a healthy dose of skepticism.

Infectious Peritonitis

Feline infectious peritonitis (FIP) is caused by a coronavirus. One strain (FeCV) causes a self-limiting enteric (intestinal) illness while another strain (FIPV) causes a more serious, and often fatal, disease. The strains are genetically identical; antibodies to one strain will be protective against other strains.[43] The FIPV strain, which causes the more serious disease, appears to be a mutant form of the enteric strain.[44] In its common enteric form, the virus causes a mild illness characterized by fever, vomiting, and diarrhea, or may be asymptomatic. The more serious systemic form is less prevalent and typically appears in cats with otherwise challenged immune systems. Infections are more common among kittens, but older cats can also become infected. FIP incidence is significantly higher in sexually intact males than in spayed females due to their different behavioral patterns.[45] Cats living in group confinement, and those allowed to roam outside, are most at risk. Certain purebred cats may also be at greater risk of FIP due to an inherited susceptibility.[46]

The primary mode of transmission is through the fecal-oral route. Even asymptomatic infected (carrier) cats can shed the virus. Transmission may also be possible through saliva and aerosol exposure.[47] Good hygiene practices, isolating ill cats, maintaining small family groups of cats, and the careful introduction of new cats tested for coronavirus, will assist greatly in preventing transmission. The incubation period can be quite variable, generally lasting from a few weeks to three months, and can extend over a period of years.[48] Although the virus will remain stable outside of the cat for 3-7 weeks, it can be inactivated easily by many household disinfectants.[49]

Most corona virus-infected cats will remain healthy, but between 1%-5% may develop FIP if they are unable to mount a sufficient immune response.[50] It has been estimated that 20%-25% of FIP infected cats are co-infected with FeLV, which suppresses the cellular immune response, ultimately leaving the cat vulnerable to clinical FIP.[51] Although remission has been known to occur, most cats that develop clinical signs of FIP will die within weeks to months following diagnosis; there is no adequate conventional treatment available.[52] Initial signs of FIP are variable and can range from no signs at all to fever, weight loss, conjunctivitis (pinkeye), upper respiratory signs, diarrhea, and depression.

FIP generally progresses in an effusive (wet) or non-effusive (dry) form, or both simultaneously.[53] With the wet form, there may be peritoneal or pleural effusions, causing fluids to leak into body cavities (abdominal and chest regions). One of the first signs owners may note is a distension of the abdomen and/or difficulty breathing caused by fluid accumulation. Cats may develop ocular disease (eye inflammation), anorexia, and depression.[54] The wet form progresses more rapidly than the dry form.

With the dry form, owners may note a generalized illness,

including fever, malaise, and weight loss. Approximately 40% of dry cases will have some nervous system involvement which may appear as posterior incoordination, partial paralysis leading to a lack of muscle coordination and a staggered gait, increased sensitivity, convulsions, and personality changes. In about 50%, there will be intra-abdominal signs, lesions may affect various organs, and occasionally organ failure will result.[55] The effusive form is associated with a strong humoral (antibody) response but a weak cellular immune response. The non-effusive form is associated with a non-protective inflammatory cell-mediated immune response.[56]

The Feline Infectious Peritonitis Vaccine (FIP):

The currently available FIP vaccine is a modified live intranasal type. This vaccine is problematic for several reasons. As mentioned earlier, kittens—particularly those raised in multiple-cat environments—are at greatest risk of infection. However, two doses of the vaccine are recommended at a 3-4 week interval *for cats greater than 16 weeks of age,* followed by annual revaccination. The vaccine is not effective in kittens under 16 weeks of age but "by 16 weeks of age, over 50% of kittens raised in coronavirus endemic, multiple cat environments...will already be infected with coronavirus."[57]

In general, studies have *not* demonstrated the vaccine's efficacy. The manufacturer's original field trial failed to show any significant protection against FIP when comparing vaccinated versus unvaccinated controls.[58] Other studies have found efficacy to be quite variable—dependent on the level of exposure and the strain encountered. Cats which have been previously exposed to coronavirus will not benefit from vaccination.[59] The vaccine appears to be more protective with low exposures to the virulent virus but not at all protective, and can accelerate FIP, with higher-dose exposures.[60] In effect, the vaccine appears to be sensitizing the animals, causing a more severe clinical manifestation of the disease. Apparently, it only elicits only a humoral (antibody) response when a cellular immune response is required.[61]

It is interesting to note that the current vaccine, as well as experimental modified live, inactivated, and recombinant vaccines, and immune serum or immunoglobulin, can cause antibody-dependent enhancement (ADE).[62] This means that vaccine-induced antibodies can actually facilitate a rapid systemic FIP infection.[63] The incubation period is drastically shortened (e.g. 1-2 days post-exposure), severe clinical signs appear rapidly, and mortality occurs more frequently than in unvaccinated cats.[64] The potential for ADE calls into question the advisability of using this vaccine in multiple cat environments, particularly in catteries, where exposure to high concentrations of the virulent virus is likely.[65]

The FIP vaccine is ineffective in kittens, has poor efficacy in cats, and may actually increase both the incidence and severity of the disease. For these reasons, this vaccine a poor choice.

Feline Calicivirus (FCV) and Feline Rhinotracheitis (FVR)

Feline calicivirus (FCV) and feline rhinotracheitis (FVR) are common causes of upper respiratory tract infections in cats.[66] Until recently, about 90% of feline respiratory tract infections were evenly divided between FCV and FVR. Today, FCV infections outnumber FVR, although simultaneous infections are common.[67]

There are many similarities between the two diseases. The incubation period for both ranges between 2-6 days. Both diseases are usually self-limiting and most infected cats can be expected to recover. Signs generally persist for up to ten days but a severe case of FVR may linger for up to six weeks. Both can be transmitted through aerosol droplets (e.g. sneezing), through contact with contaminated objects, and can be carried by handlers from an infected cat to a susceptible cat. The viruses can be shed from eyes, nose, and mouth for a number of months.[68] Some cats become persistently infected with FCV and can shed the virus for months to years. Chronic carrier status can arise from either infection.[69]

Signs associated with feline calicivirus include coughing, sneezing, eye and nose discharge, conjunctivitis, depression, a reduced interest in food, and ulceration of the tongue, palate, and nostrils. Diarrhea and seizures have also been associated with calicivirus infection, albeit rarely. Pneumonia has been known to develop in very young or debilitated cats. A few calicivirus strains produce a limping syndrome, along with joint tenderness, fever, and alternating leg lameness, which usually resolves without treatment.[70]

Feline rhinotracheitis is caused by feline herpesvirus type 1. Some cats will test positive for the virus but never develop clinical illness. When FVR signs do occur, they include coughing, sneezing, fever, runny nose, eye inflammation, depression and anorexia. Most cats will recover without incident. Mortality is very low, but the disease can be more serious for young kittens and older cats.

The FCV and FVR Vaccines:

FCV and FVR vaccines are generally given in combination and may also include vaccines against feline leukemia, chlamydiosis, panleukopenia, and rabies. Injectable vaccines may be of the modified live or inactivated types. Topical modified live vaccines administered intranasally, and sometimes in the eyes, are available.[71]

FCV/FVR vaccines do not prevent infection or viral shedding. Instead, they may "reduce local disease and protect vaccinated cats against serious systemic disease."[72] But many studies raise concerns over the vaccine's potential to induce disease in vaccinees and their contacts, its inability to address all field strains to which cats may be exposed, and the potential for vaccine-induced carrier states.

The vaccine viruses themselves are problematic. Although the feline calicivirus has undergone significant changes over the past few decades, vaccine manufacturers still use a strain isolated over 20 years ago that may not address current field isolates.[73] None of the available vaccines contain the strains associated with the FCV-related limping syndrome. Studies conducted on the FCV vaccine alone have demonstrated that it can cause the disease in some cats.[74] Similarly, very recently vaccinated cats may become infected with what appears to be a field, versus vaccine, strain. Certainly this indicates vaccine failure but it may also imply disease provocation due to a general vaccine-induced immune suppression.[75]

The FVR portion of the modified-live vaccine presents particular problems. The virus can be attenuated (weakened) only so much or the vaccine will become ineffective. A lower degree of attenuation, however, means that intranasal exposure can induce the disease. Even the injectable vaccines can induce the disease. For example, 12-year-old Pumpkin received a combined FCV/FVR vaccine. For the next week, she exhibited respiratory signs consistent with vaccine-induced infection, fever, lethargy, runny nose and sneezing. One wonders about the rationale behind using this vaccine since it merely seems to hasten infection rather than prevent it.

Vaccinated cats do become infected with both diseases and shed the virus as abundantly as unvaccinated cats. In fact, a recent survey examining cats with upper respiratory tract disease found that 50% of cats shedding FCV and 67% of cats shedding FVR were fully vaccinated.[76] One study noted that viral shedding persisted for up to 13 days for the FVR component while FCV was shed for up to 83 days.[77] As long as cats shed the virus, they can transmit the disease to other susceptible animals. As with natural infections, there is a concern over cats succumbing to a carrier state where they can shed the virus for an indeterminate period of time.

FCV/FVR vaccines are generally administered in combination with other vaccines, increasing the likelihood of adverse effects. While testing two different modified live injectable vaccines, it was found that concurrent vaccination with *either* the rabies vaccine *or* the feline leukemia virus vaccine increased short term reactions by 2.6 times and 7.2 times, respectively.[78] When *both* rabies and FeLV vaccines were administered with the test vaccines, the short term reaction rate increased 8.9-fold. Delayed reactions, including pain, lethargy, fever, or anorexia occurring 7-21 days (the duration of the study) post-vaccination, were doubled when cats received *any* concurrent vaccination.[79] Anaphylaxis, conjunctivitis, sneezing, nasal discharge, and inflammation of the eyes, sinuses and nose were also noted following vaccination. Reactions were significantly higher in cats one year of age and older whether or not other vaccines were administered simultaneously. Although annual revaccination is recommended, this presents an unnecessary risk in terms of adverse events. Vaccine-induced immunity should endure for at least three years and likely over seven years.[80]

Essentially, the FCV/FVR vaccine will not prevent infection nor will it have any positive effect on viral shedding. Potential adverse reactions include: fever, sneezing, conjunctivitis, eye and nose discharge, lameness, viral shedding, and vaccine-induced infection.[81] Transient sneezing may occur 4-7 days following intranasal vaccination, and oral or nasal ulceration may be observed.[82]

Bordetella

Feline Bordetella Bronchiseptica (FeBb) bacteria has only recently been recognized as a pathogen affecting cats, so there is still much to learn. FeBb causes a respiratory tract infection that is virtually indistinguishable from feline calicivirus and rhinotracheitis, unless the antigen is isolated and specifically identified.

FeBb is transmitted through the intranasal or aerosol route. Signs include a mild fever, sneezing, eye and nose discharge, and occasional coughing. In severe cases, pneumonia may develop. Many cats will harbor bordetella but will remain completely healthy. Others, presumably due to weakened immune systems, become ill. Co-infection, environment (e.g. over-crowding), nutrition, stress, and hygiene will all influence the cat's ability to mount an effective immune response. Although exposure to bordetella is common, there is no data indicating how frequently exposed cats become ill.[83] Antibiotics may be advised but since FeBb can be confused with viral respiratory illnesses, they should only be used if *clearly* indicated.

The Feline Bordetella Bronchiseptica Vaccine (FeBb):

There is only one FeBb vaccine available, and at the time of writing it appears to be licensed only in the U.S. This live intranasal vaccine is recommended for healthy cats four weeks of age or older. Since this is a relatively new vaccine, independent studies on safety and efficacy are lacking. The American Association of Feline Practitioners (AAFP) states that trials conducted by the manufacturer prior to licensure indicate that vaccinated cats "experienced less severe signs of disease than did unvaccinated controls when challenge exposed three weeks after vaccination."[84] Studies determining duration of immunity have not been completed. Presently, the AAFP does *not* recommend routine vaccination. They suggest that it may be considered for multiple-cat environments (e.g. shelters, catteries, etc.) where the disease has been confirmed, but they caution that "the ability of this product to reduce the prevalence of infection or the severity of disease in such environments has not been evaluated."[85] As with any new vaccine, actual safety and efficacy will not be known until the vaccine becomes widely used.

Chlamydiosis

Feline chlamydiosis (Pneumonitis) is a bacterial infection caused by *Chlamydia psittaci*. The bacteria can be transmitted through the air, by cat handlers, or *possibly* via inanimate objects. Conjunctivitis is the most common sign, but sneezing, fever, and nasal discharge may develop. Conjunctivitis can be chronic and recurring. (Special care should be taken when handling infected cats as C. psittaci conjunctivitis can be transmitted to humans as well.) Signs generally appear 5-10 days after exposure, with the course of the disease lasting about 30 days. Studies have estimated that 5%-10% of the general cat population has been exposed to C. psittaci.[86] Most cases are found in cats five weeks to nine months of age.

The disease is relatively mild; treatment is largely supportive and symptomatic. Frequent removal of eye and nasal discharge will greatly improve the cat's comfort. A clean cloth, dampened with warm water, will help soften and remove dry exudate. Antibiotics, such as tetracycline, may be prescribed. Bland antibiotic eye ointments, applied 5-6 times per day, will prevent corneal irritation.[87]

The Feline Chlamydiosis (C. Psittaci) Vaccine:

Both modified live and inactivated vaccines containing adjuvants (antibody boosters) are available, often in combination with rhino-tracheitis, calicivirus, panleukopenia, and sometimes rabies. The vaccine will not prevent infection but it is said to protect cats from the more severe manifestations of the disease. The C. psittaci vaccine is known to cause a higher rate of adverse reactions than most other feline vaccines. These include "lethargy, depression, anorexia, lameness, and fever, 7 to 21 days after vaccination."[88] One study also determined that if the vaccine is accidentally administered into the eye, e.g. by aerosolized droplets during vaccine reconstitution, cats will develop clinical Chlamydia disease and shed C. psittaci.[89]

In one household, two unrelated kittens were adopted at the same time. Mymble had been vaccinated but Peri had not. Both, however, became infected with the disease as a result of Mymble's vaccination. Within a few weeks, the kittens developed conjunctivitis and began sneezing. Peri recovered well but Mymble continued to have eye problems. The vaccine-induced disease did not stop there, however, as their owner also became infected and was treated with a lengthy course of antibiotics. Feline-to-human transmission does not appear to be a common event but it certainly can occur.

Although the AAFP suggests that the feline chlamydia vaccine may be considered in the case of multiple-cat environments where the clinical disease has been confirmed, they do *not* recommend its routine use due to concerns associated with adverse events, due to the mild nature of the disease, and because available treatments will produce a favorable response.[90]

Panleukopenia

Feline panleukopenia (FPL) is caused by a parvovirus. While the disease is often referred to as *feline distemper*, it is not related to canine distemper. It may also be referred to as *feline infectious enteritis* or *feline parvovirus*. The virus is virtually indistinguishable from mink enterovirus and is very closely related to canine parvovirus type 2, both of which appear to have descended from the feline virus.[91] The virus is fairly widespread; most outdoor cats will be exposed to it within the first year of life.

The incubation period for FPL is generally between 2-10 days. Most FPL infections are subclinical and cats will remain healthy. When the clinical disease does develop, signs can include fever, depression, anorexia, vomiting, diarrhea, a swollen and tender abdomen, and extreme dehydration, usually for a period of 5-7 days. Infected kittens that are no longer protected by maternal antibodies, or who may have been infected in utero, may be at risk of cerebellar hypoplasia (a deficiency of brain cells), lack of coordination, tremors, and retinal lesions. Between 25% and 90% die within days of the onset of signs.[92] Spontaneous abortions and stillbirths may result if the queen is infected during pregnancy. Long-term sequelae include anemia, hypoglycemia, and hypo-proteinemia.

Transmission of the virus generally occurs by the fecal-oral route, but in acutely ill cats the virus may be shed via any bodily secretion. The virus can survive, and remain infectious, in the feces of recovered cats for six weeks. The virus can also survive on contaminated objects or clothing, but it can be neutralized with bleach. Treatment is largely supportive, but serious signs will warrant additional care. It is extremely important to keep ill cats well-hydrated and to provide vitamin supplementation.

The Feline Panleukopenia Vaccine (FPL):
Feline panleukopenia vaccines are available in either intranasal, injectable modified live, or inactivated forms, and are generally administered in combination with other vaccines. The vaccines are considered to be very effective in preventing both infection and clinical disease. Immunity is expected to endure for more than seven years.[93] Therefore, the AAFP recommends that, *"following the initial series, and revaccination one year later, cats should be vaccinated no more frequently than once every three years."*[94]

Modified live FPL vaccines should be avoided in kittens less than four weeks old, pregnant queens, and cats that are ill or immunosuppressed, due to the potential for vaccine-induced infection. One breeder noted that, in 20 years, the *only* case of feline pankeukopenia she observed was in a kitten recently given the modified live vaccine. Within a few days of vaccination, the newly adopted kitten was returned to her dying. The kitten had not been in contact with any ill animal nor been outside. A next-generation kitten from the same line demonstrated immune deficiencies so it is quite likely that the first kitten may have been similarly affected.

In an early study involving ferrets, it was found that when 1-2 day old kits were vaccinated with FPL, they developed cerebral hypoplasia, marked by gross lesions to the cerebellum or a significant reduction in the size of the cerebellum, and demonstrated general motor impairment, tremors, and loss of righting and climbing abilities.[95] Pregnant feline queens run the risk of vaccine-induced abortion or birth defects in the kittens. Vaccination is not recommended before 12 weeks of age due to the vaccine-neutralizing effect of maternal antibodies. The AAFP has suggested that the intranasal vaccine may not be as effective as the injectable vaccines in kittens.[96]

It must also be understood that if the animal is vaccinated at the same time as surgery, the immune system will be over-burdened, increasing the potential for adverse reactions. This may also serve to prime the animal for an even stronger vaccine reaction in the future. For example, Yoda, a Russian blue, was neutered at the same time as he received a combined vaccine containing panleukopenia, calicivirus, rhinotracheitis and chlamydia. His owners noted that he was lethargic, weak, dizzy and nauseated. Within a week, Yoda began vomiting several times each day. After receiving the same vaccines the following year, Yoda again became weak, feverish, disoriented, vomited blood and had bloody diarrhea. His veterinarian suggested that Yoda had developed IBD (irritable bowel disease). Yoda's owners report that he has become a bit more jumpy, twitching when his back is touched, and has developed allergies to many things. Yoda is now under the care of a holistic veterinarian and his vomiting episodes have been reduced to a few times per month. Clearly, careful consideration must be given to the immune status of an animal before this, or any other, vaccine is administered.

Feline Rabies

Cats experience *furious* rabies more often than *dumb* rabies. (See page 49 for an explanation.) However, temperament changes may be quite subtle until the disease progresses.[97] If that occurs, the cat may become aggressive and experience muscle tremors, ataxia, increased salivation, convulsions, paralysis, coma, and death.[98]

Typically, there are about 100-300 feline rabies cases reported in the U.S. per year. From 1946-1995 there were just ten cases of human rabies reported from exposure to rabid cats.[99] In recent years, rabies incidence in cats has increased considerably, and at times outnumbers incidence in dogs. This is primarily because of the high number of stray cats that migrate between farms—helping to reduce the rodent population—but are never cared for as pets.[100] Exposure to rabies through contact with wild animals is increased for strays. The natural exposure potential for pet cats is minimal, and for housebound cats, nonexistent. Vaccination appears to present the major risk of contracting rabies for pet cats.

The Feline Rabies Vaccine:
The frequency with which vaccine-induced rabies occurs is not a matter of public record. As one study states: "The Atlanta Centers for Disease Control (CDC) has investigated many instances of apparent vaccine-induced rabies, which are not in the literature."[101] It appears, however, that vaccine-induced rabies occurs more often in cats than dogs, and more often in young animals than adults.[102]

In one study, four cats contracted atypical rabies. Tests definitively revealed the causal strain was from the modified live ERA-strain rabies vaccines the cats received 13-17 days prior to the onset of paralysis.[103] In at least two of the cats, paralysis began in the vaccinated limb; details describing the vaccination sites for the other two cats were unavailable. The cases were considered to be atypical due to prolonged survival times (although each was euthanized), rigid hyperextension of the limbs, and no difficulties with swallowing. Two of the cats were apparently not even at risk of contracting rabies naturally as they "were from a county that had no reported natural rabies in over 20 years."[104] The effects of this tragedy went beyond the untimely deaths of the cats: more than 50 people suffered rabies prophylaxis treatment because they were exposed to the animals. Inactivated vaccines appear to elicit a better immune response, and induce fewer cases of rabies in cats, than modified live vaccines.[105]

The rabies vaccine also presents a considerable cancer risk. For example, Autumn, a 12-year-old grey and white domestic short hair cat, received a rabies vaccine. Within seven months, she developed a fibrosarcoma at the vaccination site. The tumor was removed but two more appeared in its place, to be followed by another directly behind, one on the left ribs, and at least ten more smaller tumors on the right ribs. After three rounds of surgery and nearly three years of struggling with vaccine-associated sarcomas, Autumn died. Her owner has since diligently tried to address the issue of vaccine safety with her political advocates but, so far, to no avail.

Sadly, Autumn's experience is not at all unusual. In 1987, Pennsylvania mandated rabies vaccinations for cats. Between 1987 and 1991, researchers at the University of Pennsylvania School of

Veterinary Medicine discovered a significant increase in feline inflammatory reactions and fibrosarcomas arising in vaccination sites.[106] Of the 198 fibrosarcomas evaluated in 1991 alone, 42 contained "gray-brown granular to crystalline foreign material... within macrophages in the inflammatory foci."[107] Three sarcomas were evaluated and found to be comprised of aluminum and oxygen, suggesting that a common aluminum-based vaccine-adjuvant was implicated in the development of sarcomas. They stated:

> Our interpretation is that the persistence of the inflammatory and immunological reactions associated with the presence of the aluminum in the injection sites predisposed the cat to a derangement of its fibrous connective tissue repair response, eventually leading to neoplasia in some of these cases.[108]

This study did not go so far as to definitively implicate aluminum as the cause of the sarcomas but merely presented the possibility. Nonetheless, it is striking to note that while there were 198 feline fibrosarcomas implicated with rabies vaccination *in Pennsylvania alone*, there were a total of 189 cases of feline rabies reported *in the entire United States* for 1991.[109]

As noted in the previous section on canine rabies (page 51), subcutaneous injection of rabies vaccine has led to focal necrotizing granulomatous panniculitis in cats as well.[110] This is a known reaction. Biopsies were taken from eight cats (and two dogs). In four of the ten specimens taken, a globular grey-brown material (likely remnants of the vaccine adjuvant) were found in the central necrotic (tissue death) zones. Biopsy sites healed within a few weeks except in one animal which developed complications in the form of a tumor-like mass.

Requirements for vaccinating pet cats against rabies are wholly unfounded. Cases generally arise in cats that are not kept as pets; they would not be vaccinated anyway. The risk that your vaccinated pet cat will succumb to vaccine-induced rabies, cancer, and/or necrotizing granulomatous panniculitis, is significant, and certainly outweighs the likelihood of contracting rabies naturally.

Ringworm

A new vaccine for this skin ailment is not recommended because it will not prevent ringworm nor hasten recovery as a treatment.[111,112] The adjuvant carries a risk of vaccine-induced sarcomas.[113]

Vaccine-Induced Sarcomas

Vaccine-induced feline sarcomas have been known to develop following a variety of vaccines, but the prevalence was not considered to be "statistically significant."[114] This scenario changed recently. Most studies indicate that these soft-tissue sarcomas develop anywhere from a few months to about 3½ years following vaccination, although longer periods have been reported. The FeLV and rabies vaccines are usually implicated.[115] Depending upon the study, it is estimated that vaccine-induced sarcomas occur in the range of 1/1000 to 1/10,000 FeLV or rabies vaccines administered. Using conservative figures, this means that up to 22,000 vaccine-induced tumors occur in cats *annually* in the U.S.[116] In countries that do *not* routinely use these vaccines, "vaccine-induced sarcomas are not recognized."[117]

In 1985, two new inactivated aluminum-adjuvant vaccines for FeLV and rabies were introduced and have been widely used. Typically, chronic inflammation will precede tumor development at the vaccination site. Examination of the tumors frequently demonstrates the presence of aluminum.[118] Inflammation has been known for many decades to be an important precursor to the development of several types of tumors.[119] Researchers do not understand why this occurs, nor what role aluminum has in the development of vaccine-induced sarcomas. From a scientific standpoint, investigators are unsure whether the aluminum actually causes the tumor or whether it is merely a marker, or residue, and other vaccine components are at fault.[120]

In a recent Utah study, 176 sarcomas were examined.[121] A "bluish-foreign material [was observed] in inflammatory macrophages associated with many of the sarcomas..."[122] In this study, no single vaccine was implicated, but a variety of feline vaccines (rabies and non-rabies) produced by multiple manufacturers. "This information suggests that some common factor such as a commonly used adjuvant is the underlying source of the problem."[123]

The route, site, vaccine-type, and number of vaccines given at a particular site, will influence the potential for tumor development. It has been suggested that subcutaneous, versus intramuscular, injection of the rabies vaccine will lead to more fibrosarcomas.[124] In another study, it was determined that not only was the FeLV vaccine implicated more often in tumor development, but injection in the cervical/interscapular site (between the shoulder blades) increased the risk.[125] A comparison was made between cats who received no vaccines in the cervical/interscapular site versus those receiving either one, two, three or more vaccines in this region. For cats receiving one vaccine, the risk of developing fibrosarcomas at the site was almost 50% higher than cats vaccinated elsewhere. The risk increased with the number of vaccines given: for two vaccines the risk was about 127% higher and for 3-4 vaccines the risk was approximately 175% higher.[126] Furthermore, the development of tumors was hastened, taking an average of 340 days to develop in the cervical/interscapular region versus 1,506 days (about four years) for all other locations.[127] Although metastasis (cancer cells spreading to distant areas) was not observed in this study, the tumors were found to be rather aggressive, with a tendency to recur after surgical excision, and the prognosis was deemed to be "guarded to poor."[128] While metastasis is not frequently observed with vaccine-induced sarcomas, it has occurred in cats with either recurrent or non-recurrent injection-site sarcomas.[129] The risk of metastasis appears to increase if there is a delay in removing tumors.[130]

Treatment costs for vaccine-induced fibrosarcomas can be exorbitant. When Bessy, a grey and white domestic short hair, was four years old, she received a rabies vaccine. Nearly four years later a tumor developed at the injection site. The biopsy confirmed rabies-vaccine induced fibrosarcoma. While Bessy's treatment is ongoing, she has endured surgery once to remove the tumor and has had 19 radiation treatments. *So far, the direct costs have come to $6376.* Her owner contacted the manufacturer, requesting assistance to cover the expenses incurred as a direct result of their vaccine, but they have failed to respond. Currently, it appears that only one manufacturer has an official strategy for partially reimbursing expenses resulting from their vaccine, and claims must be initiated through the veterinarian.

Although the FeLV and rabies vaccines have received the most attention, other vaccines can cause cancer. Sylvia, a 12-year-old domestic short hair, developed a tumor at the site where she had been vaccinated less than one month earlier. Sylvia had only received vaccines against respiratory diseases. Within a month of its discovery, the tumor had greatly increased in size and was excised. For the following ten months, Sylvia seemed to be doing well but the tumor returned. Within four months, the lemon-sized tumor appeared as several connected masses and began ulcerating her skin. Sylvia's comfort was severely impaired by this time, necessitating euthanasia.

A retrospective study was initiated to determine whether there was an association between inactivated panleukopenia and respiratory virus vaccines and the development of tumors.[131] The investigation was prompted by the observation of a recurrent fibrosarcoma in a cat in the interscapular region where the yearly panleukopenia and respiratory virus vaccines had been administered. Upon review of laboratory data spanning more than ten years, it was found that the risk of tumor development was 1.3 cases per 1,000 cats vaccinated.[132] The actual incidence rate may well have been higher since estimates were based upon the number of vaccines purchased in the local region, the number of recall notices, and computer-generated billing records, which may not have adequately accounted for wastage.

Most sarcomas were discovered between 3-19 months following vaccination, although some owners reported having noticed nodules immediately after vaccination. Tumors tended to recur following excision and, in some cases, they recurred before the sutures were removed. Of 14 cats studied, there was an average of three tumor recurrences, with the range falling between zero and eight recurrences.[133] Eight cats were euthanized because of multiple recurrences.

Authors of this study noted that any determination regarding the role of adjuvants in tumor development was frustrated because they simply could not access information from the manufacturers. Both researchers and veterinarians are in the precarious position of administering products without having full knowledge of the ingredients. Still, once they switched to a modified live vaccine, replacing the killed vaccine for their practice, "no new cases of interscapular sarcoma [were] diagnosed."[134] The authors noted that while continuously using the same site for vaccination may create an initiator/promoter sequence (i.e. cause multiple insults leading to changes required for tumor development), it appeared that the use of the killed vaccine was the most important factor.[135]

Vaccine-induced sarcomas furnish yet another important reason to carefully weigh vaccine-related benefit and risks. For indoor cats, the risk of sarcoma development may outweigh any perceived benefit of vaccination. For other cats, the risk may still be too high and should be properly assessed based upon disease incidence and other potential factors that will influence their chance of exposure. Clearly, repeated vaccination in the same area increases the potential for excessive inflammatory reactions and the development of sarcomas. The risk appears to be amplified when vaccinating in the interscapular region and when utilizing inactivated/killed vaccines.[136]

TABLE 2:
FELINE VACCINES

Disease	Comments
Feline Leukemia	Vaccine has variable efficacy and carries a high risk for fibrosarcomas. Not recommended for low-risk cats or those greater than four months old.
Feline Immunodeficiency Virus	Vaccine offers no protection against infection and will enhance viral replication in exposed cats.
Infectious Peritonitis	Ineffective vaccine increases incidence and severity of the disease. Vaccinated cats develop severe infectious peritonitis faster, and die more frequently, than unvaccinated cats.
Calicivirus and Rhinotracheitis	Vaccines will not prevent infection or shedding. May induce disease and carrier state. Adverse events are increased in cats one year and older, and in those receiving feline leukemia (FeLV) or rabies vaccines simultaneously.
Bordetella Bronchiseptica	New vaccine: safety and efficacy are not established.
Chlamydiosis (Pneumonitis)	Vaccine will not prevent infection, has a high adverse reaction rate, and may cause the clinical disease. Natural disease is mild and treatments are effective.
Panleukopenia	Vaccine-induced infection risk for cats less than four weeks old and immunosuppressed or pregnant cats. Spontaneous abortion and birth defects are possible, as well as brain damage.
Rabies	Rabies risk for pet cats is low; for indoor cats, nonexistent. Vaccine can induce rabies, paralysis, and carries a high fibrosarcoma risk.
Ringworm	Vaccine is not recommended for routine use because it will not prevent ringworm. The vaccine is sometimes used as a treatment after infection, but there is no convincing evidence of its efficacy. The adjuvant carries a risk of vaccine-induced sarcomas.

Holistic Pet Care Options

Many pet owners are discovering the benefits of holistic veterinary care. Natural health care modalities offer your pet viable alternatives to vaccines and conventional drugs. In this chapter, some holistic pet care options will be introduced and summarized. These include: nutrition, herbs, acupuncture, chiropractic, and homeopathy. Valuable resources may be found here as well.

Nutrition and Herbs

All pet foods are not equal. In fact, some commercially prepared foods are actually dangerous to the health and well-being of our pets. Ann Martin has done exceptional research in this area. In her books, *Food Pets Die For* and *Protect Your Pet: More Shocking Facts*, Martin reports on the inferior ingredients and toxins found in many commercially prepared pet foods. For example, drugged and diseased animals may be ground up for use in some pet foods. Although the food may be exposed to high temperatures for sterilization, this may have a detrimental effect on the nutritional value of the final product. If the nutrients have been destroyed, or they are technically present but not in a form that can be digested, vitamin deficiencies are possible.

A diet of natural, often raw, foods will enhance your pet's health. *Dr. Pitcairn's Complete Guide to Natural Health for Dogs & Cats* provides a comprehensive yet easy-to-follow guide simplifying the transition from commercial foods with little or no value to homemade foods with excellent nutritional merit. What your pet ingests determines how well his entire body is able to function—including the ability of his immune system to fight off disease.

Herbal medicine is another very effective healing modality. Sick animals in the wild will frequently eat medicinal plants to maintain and restore health. Although herbs are commonly used in many pharmaceutical preparations, typically the *whole* plant is not used; some beneficial parts that work synergistically are absent. Pharmaceuticals often include many undesirable compounds as well.

Herbs have a wide range of uses. For example, echinacea enhances the immune system, raspberry leaf is for uterine balance and birthing, garlic is a natural antibiotic, valerian root is a relaxant, and chamomile promotes sleep. The challenge with herbs occurs when an animal requires prolonged treatment and she dislikes the taste. Pet owners must become creative. Also, because herbs are strong medicine, they should be administered with caution under the supervision of an experienced herbalist. Some herbs that may be wholly beneficial to humans could have a toxic effect on pets. When administered properly, however, herbs can strengthen the body and offer solutions to many illnesses that are poorly treated by conventional medicine.

Acupuncture

Veterinary acupuncture has been used in China for almost 4,000 years. The American Academy of Veterinary Acupuncture (AAVA) advocates the use of acupuncture to assist the animal's body in healing itself. Veterinary acupuncture is used to "stimulate nerves, increase blood circulation, relieve muscle spasms, and cause the release of hormones," such as endorphins or cortisone (to naturally control pain).[1] Acupuncture has many applications. It can be effective in the prevention and treatment of neurological, gastrointestinal, urinary, dermatological, and musculoskeletal disorders.

Chiropractic

Back problems are not the only health issue benefited by chiropractic adjustments. Nerves travel throughout the body. If vertebrae are misaligned, and major nerve cords are compressed (subluxated), diverse afflictions are possible. Efficient functioning of the entire body will be enhanced by a properly adjusted spine.

A few years ago, I witnessed a dramatic testament to the benefits of chiropractic, massage therapy, patterning, and the determination of a devoted pet owner. My brother, Tony, had a six-year-old Doberman pinscher named Taviar who developed Wobbler's Syndrome, a hereditary ailment generally described as cervical disc compression with lameness gradually appearing in the hind limbs then progressing to the front limbs. In Taviar's case, the onset was acute. He was completely well one day then paralyzed the next. The prognosis was guarded-to-poor; his veterinarian recommended euthanasia if no improvement was noted within a week.

Taviar lost considerable weight during that week and his muscles were clearly atrophying. He could eat but not stand, and required assistance to defecate. Tony massaged Taviar twice per day and began patterning, a type of physiotherapy imitating walking movements. Within a week, Taviar could stand if he leaned on Tony. At that point, Taviar received a chiropractic adjustment. The improvement was dramatic. Continuing with the regimen, Taviar stood unassisted within another 4-6 weeks. Soon thereafter, he began walking, relearned to climb stairs, and was again able to run. The combination of chiropractic, massage therapy, patterning, patience, and love gave Taviar another year of quality life.

Chiropractic also helped my cat, Benjamin, who missed the mark when it came to agility. He would jump on furniture, only to fall off. After he was adjusted, his "clumsiness" stopped. Furthermore, once he understood what was happening during adjustments, he became very settled and seemed to enjoy the procedure.

Homeopathy

Homeopathy provides a variety of *remedies* and *nosodes* that are effective in the prevention and treatment of disease, and, in fact, in the treatment of many vaccine-induced adverse events. Nosode use is generally considered to be optimal at the time of exposure, or shortly thereafter. Homeopaths have found them to be quite effective, even in shelter situations. Although some homeopaths may not use nosodes as preventives, others will use them as preventives during critical periods. For example, Dr. Don Hamilton, DVM, author of *Homeopathic Care for Cats and Dogs,* notes that he will use "30C (low) potencies once or twice a week until the animal is six to eight months old," then stop preventive nosode administration.[2] After this age, he feels that continuing nosodes as a preventive is unnecessary and potentially detrimental, unless exposure is imminent. Dr. Susan Beal, DVM, a holistic veterinarian in Pennsylvania, explains the prophylactic use of nosodes as "filling a chink in the armor through which the naturally occurring disease would have entered."[3] Nosodes induce a medicinal disease state in the patient that is similar to the natural disease. "As such, the two diseases cannot occupy the same space at the same time—the nosode thus prevents the naturally occurring disease from taking hold."[4] Unlike vaccination, however, homeopathy does not utilize a "blanket approach." All protocols are uniquely designed for each patient.

Homeopathy provides individualized care based not only upon the symptoms, but on the entire circumstances of the patient. Thus, it is advisable to consult with a professional homeopath to ensure that the protocol will be most effective. Doctors Patty Smith and Rudi Verspoor, of Ottawa's Hahnemann Center Clinic, have had great success using homeopathy for both disease prevention and treatment of vaccine injuries. When discussing their protocol for treating humans and animals with vaccine injuries, they noted that they generally approach the most recent pathology first and then work backwards, taking into account the patient's mental, physical, and emotional integrity. By the time they reach the deepest layers associated with the symptomology, the patient often experiences complete recovery, or at the very least, a significant improvement in their quality of life. This approach is in contrast to the use of allopathic drugs which may provide symptomatic relief yet carry a high potential for side effects. Of course, when treating vaccine-induced injuries, outcome will depend upon the level of damage. Thus it is important to work closely with your health practitioner to obtain the most successful protocol for your pet.

Resources

The *Animal Natural Health Center* (www.drpitcairn.htm) was founded by Richard Pitcairn, DVM as a clinical and teaching center for the understanding and use of homeopathic medicine to treat disease. They also emphasize the use of excellent nutrition using home-prepared and raw foods. They offer training and information for veterinarians and others interested in true healing for animals.

The *Thinktwice Global Vaccine Institute* (www.thinktwice.com) offers parents and other concerned people educational resources enabling them to make more informed vaccine decisions. *Thinktwice* encourages an unbiased exchange of vaccine information, and supports every family's right to accept or reject vaccines. In addition, they offer a very large selection of uncensored vaccine information, including up-to-date vaccination laws, vaccine books, and other hard to find vaccine resources imported from around the world.

Ethical & Legal Considerations

In this chapter, several principles related to vaccine safety and veterinary obligations will be examined. These include: informed consent, implied contract, adverse event reporting, conflicts of interest, negligence, malpractice, liability and compensation.

Informed Consent

Ethical guidelines and legislation governing veterinary practices are nearly the same as those governing medicine for human patients. Like any medical practitioner, the veterinarian must obtain consent for any intervention *except* in an emergency situation where it may not be possible and delay would seriously harm the patient. Consent must be provided by an individual who is mentally and legally capable. For consent to be valid, it must be informed and given voluntarily.

Consent is more than the act of signing a form allowing a particular procedure to be carried out. A signed consent form will not convince any court that the client was adequately informed; it serves only to verify that a particular procedure was permitted. Informed consent is a *process* whereby the expert discloses the nature of the treatment, its associated risks and benefits, appropriate alternatives, and the expected outcome for proposed courses of action. Client questions must be answered and any information that would potentially change the client's decision should be disclosed. It is never acceptable to withhold information because a client may refuse a proposed intervention, even if the professional believes that the intervention is in the patient's best interest.

When a veterinarian agrees to care for an animal, an implied contract is created. Part of this contract assumes that the veterinarian is aware of the potential risks associated with any intervention and that these are disclosed to the client *prior* to consent. It has often been the case that rare or merely possible (versus probable) risks have not been disclosed. Sadly, this lack of disclosure has been supported by law. More recently, however, cases have arisen in the courts requiring that even rare risks be disclosed.[1] For the protection of the practitioner—and benefit of the client and patient—it is far better to provide more, rather than less, information.

In all of Canada, and about half of the United States, the medical practitioner is required to disclose "the amount and kind of information that a *reasonable patient* would find material to making a decision about treatment."[2] In the remaining states, disclosure is based upon the type and amount of information that a *reasonable physician* would disclose.[3] While the former method is clearly more advantageous for the client, neither method provides any clear formula for determining exactly what must be disclosed and what legitimately can be omitted. This is particularly true of vaccination since the results of many studies are conflicting and there is little opportunity for veterinarians to access information on the types and frequency of serious adverse events. If this information is not easily accessible, how can veterinarians provide sufficient information to their clients?

As the learned intermediary between the manufacturer and the client, the veterinarian is placed in a legally vulnerable position. The client must make a decision without adequate information. If a veterinarian fails to disclose potential risks, and the animal is subsequently harmed, the veterinarian can be sued.[4] However, as long as the veterinarian warns of the potential for a specific adverse event, if that event does occur, the veterinarian cannot be held liable unless injuries are the result of negligence.[5]

Immunization protocol forms, written in plain language, are a very good idea to protect veterinarians. Clients (*you!*) and patients (*your pet!*) gain from full disclosure. Standard forms explaining both the risks and benefits of vaccination, applicable vaccination legislation, the prevalence of certain diseases within the region, as well as available treatments and their expected outcomes, should be supplied to each client *prior* to the vaccination appointment. It should be remembered that consent necessarily involves dialogue. Any printed materials are merely *a starting-point* to the disclosure process; they are not equivalent to this process.

Adverse Event Reporting

Inadequate adverse event reporting is one serious obstacle to adequate disclosure. Serious adverse events can occur from any vaccine. In order to properly identify adverse event trends, it is vital that adverse event reporting be made mandatory and that these reports are investigated. The resulting information must then be disseminated to both veterinarians and the public. As with human vaccine-associated adverse event reporting, the veterinary scene falls short of the ideal.

In Canada, the Veterinary Biologics & Biotechnology Section (VBBS) of the Canadian Food Inspection Agency (CFIA) is the regulatory body responsible for licensing veterinary biologics and for receiving adverse event reports. The vaccine manufacturers themselves are primarily responsible for investigating reported adverse events.[6] A veterinarian or pet owner can submit a report to either the CFIA or the manufacturer. The manufacturer is obligated to investigate all adverse events, but they need only report Type 1 (systemic), Type 2 (mortality), and Type 3 (persistent local reactions) to the CFIA.[7] Depending upon the nature of the reaction, the manufacturer may be required to submit a product sample to the CFIA for laboratory testing or to conduct its own additional safety studies. If a product is to be recalled or withdrawn from the market, manufacturers must provide written notification to veterinarians and other purchasers by way of a letter that has been approved by the VBBS. Although this sounds like an efficient method for tracking adverse events, there are significant problems with the Canadian adverse event reporting system. There is an enormous conflict of interest inherent with this process. Adverse event reporting obligations appear to be directed only to the manufacturer. Aside from products scheduled to be withdrawn from the market, there is no current mechanism available to disseminate adverse event information to veterinarians and the public.

A conflict of interest arises when those who are responsible for costly vaccine development, testing, marketing, and providing vaccination recommendations, are the very same people responsible for investigating post-licensure adverse event reports. Vaccines are undeniably expensive to develop and produce. As has been demonstrated time and again with vaccines developed for human use, manufacturers are extremely reluctant to acknowledge safety issues once a vaccine has been released. Recovering expenditures may well influence their perception of "acceptable losses." This could easily be rectified if an independent agency was given the responsibility of receiving and investigating all adverse event reports.

Strangely, regulations governing adverse event procedures are aimed only at the vaccine manufacturers' obligations. There is no mention of the veterinarian's duty to report vaccine-related adverse events. Thus, there is some question as to the actual percentage of reports that will even reach a manufacturer, let alone anyone else.[8]

Clearly, adverse event information does not reach the Canadian Veterinary Medical Association (CVMA), veterinarians, or the public.[9] How can veterinarians or pet owners assess whether vaccination is appropriate for individual animals if they are not informed of the types or frequency of adverse events? Understanding specific adverse event trends can serve as a warning to preclude either a certain type of animal, a certain breed, or animals with known relevant preconditions, from vaccination with an agent that will increase their risk of adverse events. That this information is not readily available is nothing less than careless endangerment. It should be said, however, that the CVMA's National Issues Committee is currently exploring a program similar to that used in the U.S.[10]

The United States' adverse event reporting system is superior, in at least some respects, to that used in Canada. Although there does not appear to be any obligation for either manufacturers or veterinarians to report adverse events, these are handled by the U.S. Pharmacopeia (USP), a non-profit third party.[11] The USP was established in 1820 to set standards for drugs and related technologies.[12] Although they initially focused only upon products for human use, in 1994 the USP developed a Veterinary Practitioners' Reporting Program (VPR) in conjunction with the American Veterinary Medical Association (AVMA). Adverse event information is entered into the USP's database and shared with the manufacturer, the appropriate regulatory agency, and the AVMA.[13] Most importantly, this information can be accessed by veterinarians. Reporting veterinarians may also be given the opportunity to participate in important studies that can provide insight into the risk factors associated with particular adverse events. For example, between March 1998 and March 1999, 190 veterinarians reported vaccine-associated sarcomas in cats. They were asked to contribute their experience and knowledge to an epidemiologic study funded by the Vaccine-Associated Feline Sarcoma Task Force "to determine risk factors for sarcoma development."[14] It is this sort of collaboration that will effectively influence vaccine recommendations, identify risk factors associated with certain vaccines, pinpoint which vaccines may need to be changed or withdrawn, determine potential reactions associated with combining certain vaccines, alert veterinarians to other potential problems, and lead to effective treatments.

Negligence, Malpractice, Liability and Compensation

Negligence occurs when there is a "breach of a legal duty to take care which results in damage" caused by "conduct which falls below the standard required in particular circumstances in order to protect others against unreasonable risk of harm, as opposed to some risk of harm."[15] In other words, there must be some legally viable duty to protect others from harm, a failure to do so, and injury resulting from that failure.

Malpractice is seen as "an extension of the law of negligence" in that it is "the failure of the veterinarian to use the requisite degree of care and skill possessed and demonstrated by other reputable veterinary medical practitioners." It may also include professional misconduct and illegal or immoral conduct.[16] Malpractice is not merely the failure of a procedure or existence of an injury. It is the fault of the practitioner lacking knowledge and/or expertise that would be expected of others in the profession. Still, whatever the result, as long as the intervention was performed in good faith, and is one that is recognized as appropriate by others in the profession, there is no negligence.[17]

In Canada, "veterinary practitioners are obliged to exercise the care, skill, and diligence provided by a reasonable practitioner in similar circumstances."[18] If an animal suffers an adverse event from a vaccine, the veterinarian would not be deemed negligent as long as he or she administered the vaccine according to recommendations and his or her actions fell within an appropriate standard of care. However, a veterinary practitioner would be considered negligent if he or she "violated the contraindication enclosed with a vaccine."[19]

In the U.S., if an adverse event occurs, the plaintiff must provide direct proof that the veterinarian had a duty of care owed to the animal, that the veterinarian breached that duty, and that "that failure was the proximate cause of injury, impairment, or death; and that damages to the patient or patient's owner resulted from the negligence."[20] The plaintiff, usually through the testimony of an expert, is required to prove that the practitioner failed to provide a standard of care, or failed to have knowledge that would be expected of others in the profession, *unless* negligence is obvious (e.g. surgical implements remaining in the body post-surgery).

Until recently, in both Canada and the U.S., if negligence was determined, damages awarded by the court were limited to the market value of the animal.[21] Despite the many similarities between human and animal medical law, there are important differences when it comes to compensation for damages. Animals have long been considered as *property*, without their own inherent legal rights. Therefore, awards for damages have been restricted to their market value.[22] Damages based upon emotional suffering of the owner were never awarded and punitive damages were only rarely awarded when it could be determined that the "practitioner [had] been particularly distasteful or malicious."[23] Slowly, this trend is changing, particularly as the inherent value of companion animals becomes recognized by the courts. It is difficult to assign an economic value to many companion animals in the way that one might assess the market value of a dairy cow. Still, courts are now allowing damages for loss of companionship, mental anguish, pain and suffering, loss of protective value, et cetera.[24] Other areas of compensation may include the cost of treatment, the difference between the value of the animal before and after the injury, cost of disposition, loss of services (e.g. stud fees), and the cost of a substitute, depending upon circumstances.[25]

In any action taken, it must be understood that there are strict time limitations. The statutes of limitations are generally determined by either the province or the state. In Canada, the limitation period may be as small as six months or as long as a few years, depending upon the province. In the U.S., plaintiffs will have between 1-5 years after the injury becomes apparent to initiate an action.[26]

As it stands now, pet owners are largely responsible for any expenses incurred due to vaccine injuries. These can be significant. For example, one American veterinarian noted that treatment costs associated with rabies vaccine-induced tumors could exceed $3,000.[27] Typically, owners have reported that the *initial* surgery and tests have fallen within this range but that *total costs* for treating vaccine-induced tumors have exceeded $6,000.

Other vaccine reactions can be equally expensive to treat. For example, Glory, a seven-year-old German shepherd, fell quite ill 19 days following her boosters. She developed a high fever, stiff neck, and became paralyzed on her right side. Glory's treatment is ongoing. Currently, her medication and veterinary bills have already reached approximately $2000. One can only speculate on the actual costs associated with the diverse range of additional injuries that vaccines cause.

Since vaccines can cause injuries, even when the vaccine is administered according to recommendations, what legal protection is there for clients when their animal is seriously injured? In Canada, there is very little protection unless negligence in some form can be proven. Canadians must generally prove negligence in vaccine-injury cases. Negligence may occur, for example, if a vaccine is released that is too virulent, impotent, contaminated, or improperly stored, transported, or handled. It must be shown that the manufacturer failed to provide an average, reasonable and prudent standard of care. In Canada, the burden to prove causation and fault rests with the plaintiff.

In the U.S., on the other hand, *strict liability* legislation places the burden of proof regarding safety on the manufacturer. The product must be free from defect, or the manufacturer—and in fact anyone involved in the chain of distribution—can be sued.[28] Although vaccines are inherently dangerous, this does *not* imply that they are *defective* in the eyes of the law. "If the vaccine is produced in accordance with the USDA guidelines, recent court decisions hold the manufacturer harmless for reactions caused by vaccines."[29] Plaintiffs suing under strict liability are required to prove that a defect was present when it left the manufacturer's control, and that the defect was the proximate cause of the injury.[30] There is no need to prove fault or breach of warranty. The concept of strict liability also requires the manufacturer to disclose risks associated with the product to the purchaser. In the case of animal vaccines in the U.S., the purchaser could be either the veterinarian or the animal owner, if the latter purchases the vaccine directly. But how many pet owners are actually informed of potential adverse events, and how many adverse events are ever investigated? The following story illustrates both problems.

Little Ann, a five-year-old Beagle, had an anaphylactic reaction to the rabies vaccine. She was given adrenaline by her veterinarian who recognized this as a clear vaccine-reaction. The incident was reported to authorities but no one bothered to contact the owners or the veterinarian for follow-up. At a later appointment, Little Ann's owners were discussing her vaccine reaction with their veterinarian. The veterinarian noted that, as a selling-tool, representatives from the vaccine manufacturing companies utilize ping pong balls and footballs as props to demonstrate the adverse tissue reactions that can be expected from their own products versus those expected from their competitors' vaccines. When was the last time this sort of demonstration was given to pet owners prior to having their pets vaccinated? Additionally, how will we ever have an adequate assessment of vaccine safety when clear adverse events are virtually ignored by authorities?

Summary and Conclusion

Less than 10% of vaccine injuries are ever reported. In practical terms, this means that we are ignorant of injury-trends associated with particular vaccines. Withdrawal of, or improvements to, specific vaccines are delayed, and identification of factors predisposing our pets to injury are not recognized. Thus, unnecessary *and preventable* adverse vaccine events in our pets will continue to occur—at least until public outrage at this fiasco mounts. I am hopeful that the pharmaceutical and veterinary industries will, in the very near future, implement favorable changes benefitting our four-legged friends.

Notes

Introduction:

1. Buttram and Hoffman, 6.
2. Recent studies on Gulf War Veterans have implicated vaccines in a significant immune imbalance whereby the antibody response is over-stimulated and the cellular response is suppressed. This imbalance has resulted in an increase in allergies, autoimmune diseases, chronic fatigue, and cancers. [Rook and Zumla, 1831-1833; McManners.]
3. In cattle, it was found that natural passive immunity is almost exclusively derived from colostrum and that mortality from infectious diseases is doubled for colostrum-deprived calves. In dogs, 96% of maternally derived antibody is transferred through the colostrum. [Pollock and Carmichael, January 1982: 37.]
4. For example, we are currently seeing many cases of measles in children less than one year of age because their vaccinated mothers cannot provide them with passive immunity against the disease.
5. Levine, 209; Essex and Kanki, 68-69. It appears that France also introduced myxomatosis into the rabbit population in 1952; the disease subsequently spread throughout Europe. [Bárcena et al., 1114.]
6. Essex and Kanki, 68-69.
7. See, for example, Kontor et al., 1697.
8. In an intriguing study testing the effects of a herpes virus vaccine on albino rabbits, it was found that rabbits vaccinated *after* exposure to the herpes virus suffered significantly higher rates of encephalitis and mortality when compared with unvaccinated herpes virus-challenged controls or with rabbits that were vaccinated prior to challenge. All but one of the unvaccinated challenged rabbits survived and recovered whereas 8 of the 20 rabbits vaccinated post-challenge died after experiencing numerous eye abnormalities, swollen and atrophied brains, and paralysis. Clearly, vaccination critically amplified the effects of viral challenge. [Narang,1984: 973-979.]
9. Personal communication, January 2, 2002.
10. Vitamin deficiencies, other than B1, also play significant roles in the advent of adverse vaccine reactions.
11. A photograph showing the reaction to Septra can be found at: [http://www. aztec-net.com/~lofrancokuvasz/Drug-Warning.htm]
12. Pollock and Carmichael, January 1982: 41.
13. Personal communication, December 16, 2000.
14. Sharp et al., 39-53.
15. For example, neither demonstrated typical close-eye responses nor the ability to adjust eye-focus upon head movement, and neither was able to direct or limit motions.
16. See, for example, Canine Distemper Vaccines.
17. Schultz, 1999.
18. Scott and Geissinger, 656-657.

19. Typically, vaccines were only tested for a few weeks or months to provide data on duration of immunity. [Scott and Geissinger, 652.]

20. American Animal Hospital Association.

21. Horzinek, 5.

22. American Animal Hospital Association.

23. Ibid.

24. Wilson, Graham S., 46. Citing M. V. Veldee.

25. Dr. Harash Narang, personal communication, April 11, 2001. As a matter of interest, it was Dr. Narang who established the connection between Bovine Spongiform Encephalopathy and its human variant Creutzfeldt-Jakob disease.

26. In 1955, for example, an improperly inactivated polio vaccine resulted in 260 cases of polio in vaccinees and their contacts; 192 were paralytic. There were 10 deaths: five among vaccinees and five among contacts of vaccinees. [Wilson, Graham S., 45-46.]

27. An additional filtration step apparently resolved this problem with inactivated FMD vaccines but it has also made the vaccine less potent, and therefore less immunogenic, as well. The VEE pandemic will be discussed in more detail later. In his article, Brown suggests replacing formaldehyde with more reliable disinfectants, such as B-propiolactone or acetylethyleneimine. Although they *may* be more reliable, like formaldehyde, they are both carcinogenic substances. [Brown, 103-104. See also, EPA and Vermint SIRI.]

28. The reactions were not limited to the family pets in this instance as their son suffered myalgic encephalomyelitis following vaccination. Needless to say, this family now refuses all vaccines. [Personal communication, July 20, 2001.]

29. The combined canine vaccine included modified live distemper, parainfluenza, adenovirus 2, parvovirus and inactivated coronavirus, with or without leptospirosis, administered intramuscularly. The involved serials also appear to have caused disease syndromes (unspecified) in nonpregnant dogs as well. In this article, authors mention the deaths of 12 pregnant bitches, 10 of which aborted after vaccination, plus the death of another dam and her five pups after receiving the vaccine. Bluetongue virus was found to be present in a number of different serials and the subsequent reports of abortions and deaths in pregnant bitches were associated with the vaccine. Subsequent studies focused primarily on transmission of the virus in utero, but not on transmission via breastmilk. [Wilbur et al., 1762-1765; Dr. Linn A. Wilbur, Head/Team Leader, Supervisory Veterinary Medical Officer, Mammalian Virology Section, Center for Veterinary Biologics-Laboratory (CVB-L), Veterinary Services (VS), Animal and Plant Health Inspection Service (APHIS), USDA, personal communication, December 22, 2000.]

30. Dr. Linn A. Wilbur, personal communication, December 22, 2000.

31. Ibid.

32. Dr. Harash Narang presents compelling arguments *against* prions as being the infective agent of BSE. Instead, he considers the infective agent to be a virus with DNA, and the existence of prion rods as resulting

from the aggregation of protease-resistant protein molecules/plaques. Another fascinating aspect presented is the distinction between scrapie strains, with one strain likely serving as the origin of BSE and interference between the strains. Infection with one strain apparently inhibits replication of the other strain which will have important implications for preventive measures. [Narang, July 2001: 642, 647-648.]

33. Ibid., 643.

34. Ibid., 643, 647.

35. One of eight hamsters injected with a 1:1000 diluted solution, heated for 15 hours, became infected with BSE. [Ibid., 646.]

36. Narang, July 2001: 651. Citing Narang, 1987.

37. Ibid., 645.

38. See, for example, Diodati, 74-80.

39. MLVs can inadvertently be inactivated, and therefore made useless, by minor temperature changes or by improper administration. [Kruth and Ellis, 423.]

40. Dr. Harash Narang, personal communication, April 11, 2001. Also see: [Narang, April 2001.]

41. The recent foot and mouth disease (FMD) epidemic in the UK, for example, appears to have been caused by the government's own laboratory in Surrey which is carrying out research on a live vaccine. This laboratory has been responsible for prior FMD outbreaks. It is interesting to note that FMD is an enteric disease and, like polio, the vaccines have been the source of many vaccine-induced infections. [Anonymous.] Official reports stating that the disease was brought into Britain via infected imported meat are implausible because the FMD strain isolated from this outbreak is the pan-Asiatic O type strain. [Anonymous.] Since "this strain is not active in any other country," but the laboratory has been conducting vaccine trials using this strain, it seems far more plausible that the epidemic was home-grown rather than imported. [Narang, April 2001.] Tragically, the response to this epidemic has been the mass-slaughter of farm animals, even though the disease is not fatal, and has extended even to animals that are not infected. When a vaccine has been offered, it has been the *modified live vaccine*, which would virtually extend the epidemic because the vaccine-virus can be excreted in feces for up to three years. [Narang, April 2001; Anonymous.] It has been suggested that a formalin-and-heat inactivated FMD vaccine could be prepared quickly and would quell this epidemic but the government is not listening. [Dr. Harash Narang, personal communication, April 11, 2001.] Dr. Narang also stated that the best option would be a "cloned vaccine, by expression, (that) contains no live virus... (because) it would also be easy to compare (and) distinguish from the wild infection by ELISA test." The distinction is important. Most countries will not import the meat from FMD-vaccinated animals because it is impossible to distinguish between the vaccine virus and the wild virus.

42. In particular, the recombinant hepatitis B vaccine has caused an enormous number of very serious adverse events, many autoimmune in

nature. A recombinant HIV vaccine was tested on HIV positive individuals in France and some of the recipients developed gaping necrotic lesions, causing premature death. For further information, see: [Diodati, 120-130, 190-191, 230-232.]

Canine

1. Johnson, 274; Siegl, 381.

2. See, for example, Parrish, 29-40; Truyen, 47-50.

3. Although no definitive statement could be made on the possibility of feline or mink vaccine viruses causing the disease in dogs, one of the six strains studied was found to be quite similar to CPV after attenuation of the virus, suggesting that further passages of the virus through cell cultures may generate the canine virus. [Tratschin, et al., 40.]

4. Siegl, 408.

5. Johnson, 275.

6. Although there was another virus isolated in 1967 and called "canine parvovirus type 1" (CPV-1), it is not related to CPV-2 discussed here. CPV-1 does not appear to cause clinical disease in dogs.

7. Dunn et al., September/October 1995: 11.

8. Brunner and Swango, 979-989.

9. Dunn et al., September/October 1995: 13.

10. The potential for infertility or birth defects has been suggested but, as yet, is not confirmed. [Aiello, 285.]

11. Dunn et al., November/December 1995: 13-16.

12. Larson and Schultz, 360.

13. Pollock and Carmichael, *Cornell Vet.* 1982: 20.

14. Carmichael, 1999: 296-297.

15. Carmichael, 1999: 297-298; Appel, 1999: 313.

16. Carmichael, 1999: 297-298; Appel, 1999: 298.

17. Larson and Schultz, 360-363.

18. Ibid., 362.

19. Dunn et al., September/October 1995: 14.

20. Appel, 1999: 313.

21. Pollock and Carmichael, January 1982: 41.

22. Carmichael, 1999: 297-298; Appel, 1999: 298.

23. Larson and Schultz, 360-363.

24. Hamilton, 359.

25. Bass et al., 912.

26. Cardiomyopathy is a disease affecting the structure and function of the heart. [Hamilton, 375.]

27. Immunosuppression has been noted following tetanus, typhoid, DPT, and Hib vaccines, for example. [Diodati, 51, 80-83.]

28. Ritter, 1160-1161. See also, Krakowka, 137-139.

29. In one study, it was found that reproductive efficiency in an Australian kennel was suddenly decreased following the appearance of CPV-2. Since only the abstract was available at the time of writing, no

further details can be included. [Gooding and Robinson, 170-174.]

30. Carmichael, 1997: 329.

31. Hamilton, 360-361.

32. Martin, 1012.

33. Hamilton, 361.

34. Martin, 1013.

35. Appel, 1999: 313; Carmichael, 1997: 329.

36. Martin, 1013; Appel, 1999: 314.

37. The CCV vaccine virus was found in the meninges of dogs with seizures and in the pancreas of dogs with acute pancreatitis. Similar adverse events were discussed in another article regarding a combined coronavirus-parvovirus attenuated vaccine. In addition, blindness, tremors, arthritis and lameness were noted. [Martin, 1013-1015; Wilson et al., 117-124.]

38. Martin, 1013.

39. Genetic material from the canine distemper virus is inserted into the canarypox virus and should cause an immune response to both viruses simultaneously. It is believed that this method will reduce, or eliminate, distemper vaccine-induced encephalitis.

40. Appel, 1999: 314; Carmichael, 1999: 302.

41. Canine distemper will sometimes be listed as a *Paramyxovirus*, which is the *family*, whereas *Morbillivirus* refers to the *genera*.

42. Pitcairn and Pitcairn, 257.

43. Aiello, 549; Blood and Studdert, 351.

44. Summers et al., 188-189.

45. Ibid., 189.

46. Blood and Studdert, 351.

47. Pitcairn and Pitcairn, 257-258.

48. Although there does not appear to be specific recommendations regarding vitamin A for use during distemper infection, it has been established that vitamin A administration can mean the difference between an uneventful recovery and complications for humans infected by measles. Vitamin A, however, must be used in appropriate doses to prevent toxicity.

49. Carmichael, 1997: 327.

50. Appel and Gillespie, 48.

51. Ibid.

52. Ibid., 48-49.

53. Ibid., 49. Citing Karzon.

54. Ibid., 49.

55. All dogs, including controls, received parvovirus vaccines. Since parvovirus is immunosuppressive, and the vaccine virus does shed, one wonders whether a completely unvaccinated control group would have experienced a more positive outcome. Unfortunately, the article does not include data regarding antibody titers prior to parvovirus vaccination but does state that distemper titers begin to decrease in all dogs at six weeks of age, which is precisely the age when the dogs were vaccinated. Further, there did not appear to be any indication that the dogs were tested

for parvovirus vaccine-induced shedding. [Chalmers and Baxendale, 349-353.]

56. Ibid., 350-351.

57. Ibid., 350.

58. Carmichael, 1999: 294.

59. See, for example, Ek-Kommonen et al., 380-383; Mori et al., September 1994: 2403-2408; Blixenkrone-Moller et al., 163-173. The above study by Mori et al., contains an important error. They attempted to determine whether clinical CDV in vaccinated dogs resulted from vaccine failure or from the emergence of a new field strain of the CD virus. While they believed that they had discovered a new field strain, it turned out that their samples were inadvertently contaminated by rinderpest, another morbillivirus. The erratum appears in the November 1994 issue on page 3285.

60. Ek-Kommonen et al., 380-381.

61. Based upon pre-publication results of this study, the most popular distemper vaccine in use at the time was withdrawn from the market. As a matter of interest, the distemper vaccines in Finland were not combined with parvovirus vaccines until February 1995. [Ibid., 380-382.]

62. Carmichael, 1999: 295.

63. Ibid., 294-295.

64. Krakowka, 139.

65. Ibid., 137-139.

66. Carmichael, 1999: 294.

67. Ibid.

68. In laboratory experiments, Carmichael found that encephalitis was a frequent occurrence 10-12 days following vaccination with the CDV/CAV-1 combination. [Ibid.]

69. McCandlish et al., 1992: 27-30.

70. Ibid., 29.

71. Thank you to Dr. F. Edward Yazbak for providing information on the prospect of transmission via licking at the injection site. Dr. Yazbak noted that, besides the fact that most veterinarians and MDs swab the injection site with alcohol, the dog's skin would be sufficiently loose, and therefore distanced from the intramuscular site, so that possibility of external leakage is extremely remote. Even if the vaccine had been administered subcutaneously, the needle would be angled in such a way that it would preclude leakage. [Personal communication, December 14, 2000.]

72. Merck, Sharp & Dohme Canada's *M-M-R II* (May 24, 1991) product insert states: "Recent studies have shown that lactating women immunized with live attenuated rubella vaccine may secrete the virus in breast milk and transmit it to breast-fed infants."

73. Revaccinating a woman who did not previously develop an adequate antibody response to rubella does not generally result in immunity. After revaccination, many of these women have experienced miscarriages. [Yazbak.] For further information on Dr. Yazbak's research, see: [http://www.garynull.com/index.htm There is a 3-part series entitled

Autism: Is there a Vaccine Connection?, as well as, *Autism 99: A National Emergency* and *Autism 2000: A Tragedy*. The documents can be located via the library search option.]

74. Foxes tend to be more severely affected than dogs. Infection can result in "acute encephalitis with convulsions followed by coma and death within 24 hours." [Philipson et al., 86.]

75. The incubation period, from exposure to onset of signs, is usually about 4-9 days. [Aiello, 561; Blood and Studdert, 548; Philipson et al., 86.]

76. Aiello, 561.

77. Goldstein, 230-231.

78. Appel, 1999: 314.

79. In one study, it was found that serum-neutralizing antibodies persisted between 7-11½ years following vaccination. However, it does not appear that challenge studies were done in this case and all dogs remained in adenovirus-free conditions. One unvaccinated control dog did develop adenovirus-specific antibodies due to exposure to the virus in the urine of the vaccinated dogs. [Fishman and Scarnell, 509.] Inactivated CAV-1 vaccines are available in Europe, and one U.S. vaccine, produced by Bayer Animal Health, contains both inactivated CAV-1 and CAV-2 components. [Appel, 1999: 314.] It appears that only modified live CAV-2 vaccines are used in Canada.

80. Carmichael, 1997: 329.

81. Ibid.

82. Carmichael, 1999: 294-295.

83. Goldstein, 79.

84. *Mycoplasma* are small bacteria-like organisms devoid of cell walls.

85. Aiello, 1125.

86. Appel, 1999: 315-316.

87. Bemis and Appel, 1085.

88. Goodnow and Shade, 597-598.

89. Appel, 1999: 315.

90. Ibid.

91. The efficacy of parenteral B. bronchiseptica vaccination has been questioned, particularly regarding formalin-killed, and non-adjuvanted, varieties. [Chladek et al., 266, 270. See also, Bemis et al., 753-762; McCandlish et al., 1976, 156-157; McCandlish et al., 1978: 51-57; Kontor et al., 1697-1698.]

92. Mucosal IgA, which is important in controlling respiratory infections, is more readily elicited by the intranasal vaccine whereas the parenteral vaccine tends to elicit circulatory IgG, but little IgG, and virtually no IgA, in the mucosa. [Goodnow and Shade, 598.]

93. Chladek et al., 266-270.

94. The authors of this study stated that B. bronchiseptica was recovered for a *shorter* period in *vaccinated* dogs, than in their unvaccinated counterparts, but their data indicates otherwise. They failed, in this instance, to account for the presence of the bacteria during the period between vaccination and challenge. This study did not include an

additional control group to examine the shedding potential of the vaccine virus and bacteria to determine the risk to susceptible contacts. [Ibid., 268-269.]

95. Wagener, 1866.

96. Carmichael, 1997: 330.

97. *Thrombocytopenia* refers to a reduction of platelets and is the most common cause of bleeding disorders. [Toshach et al., 126-128.]

98. In humans, leptospirosis was often confused with yellow fever and infectious hepatitis. It wasn't until the 1930s that it became possible to differentiate between these diseases. Contact with infected rat urine appears to be at the root of most human infections. Symptoms are similar to influenza. Jaundice may or may not be present. The disease generally resolves within a few weeks but liver or kidney damage may result in severe cases. [Parish, 146, 191; Ross, 309.]

99. Aiello, 476.

100. Appel, 1999: 317.

101. Rentko et al., 242.

102. Ross, 309; Rentko et al., 235, 242-243.

103. Diesch, 908.

104. Ibid.; Ross, 308.

105. Ross, 308.

106. Carmichael, 1997: 331.

107. Rentko et al., 241.

108. One dog had been vaccinated within a week of diagnosis and another two dogs within three months.

109. Serovars grippotyphosa and pomona are usually found in wild carnivores such as skunks, racoons and opossums. [Rentko et al., 243.]

110. Carmichael, 1997: 331.

111. Rentko et al., 242-243.

112. Ibid.; See also, Broughton and Scarnell, 311.

113. Schultz, 1982: 1148.

114. Appel, 1990: 618-619.

115. Lyme vaccines are not available for cats, horses or cattle. Cats may become infected but this is relatively rare in comparison with dogs. The disease appears to be considerably milder in cats. Clinical illness does not appear to occur in wild animals. In humans, the symptoms of Lyme disease include: joint inflammation, chills, fever, headache, malaise and skin eruptions. In severe cases, an individual may experience meningitis, Bell's Palsy, or cardiac abnormalities. [Ibid., 620; Anderson et al., 934.]

116. Appel, 1990: 622.

117. Jacobson et al., 173, 175.

118. Appel, 2000, 256.

119. Jacobson et al., 175; Appel, 1990: 622; Aiello, 436; Blood and Studdert, 681; Anderson et al., 272, 713.

120. Jacobson et al., 176.

121. Appel, 1990: 623.

122. Aiello, 437; Appel, 2000: 256-257.

123. It should be noted that the vaccine does not clear persistent infection in a dog that has already been exposed to the antigen. [Ibid.]

124. Aiello, 437.

125. Ma et al., 1370; Lim et al., 1404.

126. Prior to the development of high antibody titers to the homologous antigen, animals were at greatest risk of developing severe destructive arthritis. The risk was reduced after they developed high antibody titers *but* they were still at increased risk of developing severe arthritis if exposed to other genomic groups of B. burgdorferi.

127. Lim et al., 1404; DuChateau et al., 2541. See also, Sigal, 63-92.

128. See, for example, Livini; Dunbar.

129. Jacobson et al., 180-181.

130. Ibid., 181.

131. Ibid., 180.

132. Appel, 2000: 257.

133. Aiello, 437.

134. Appel, 2000: 256.

135. Schell.

136. Aiello, 996.

137. Green, 4.

138. Bunn, 380.

139. Esplin et al., 1993, 1246.

140. Fekadu, 1991(b): 195.

141. Dogs and cats can transmit the virus for 3-5 days before the onset of signs. Skunks can transmit the virus for up to eight days. [Aiello, 967.]

142. Ibid.

143. In experiments noted by this author, approximately 20% of experimental animals survived rabies infection even when no treatment was given. [Fekadu, 1991(b): 192.]

144. Ibid., 195.

145. Ibid., 193.

146. Jenner developed two smallpox vaccines. The first, he said, did not work. The second was refused by the public, who were disgusted with the ingredients. Jenner not only reintroduced the first vaccine but managed to convince the Royal College of Physicians and the British Parliament to impose mandatory vaccination. The smallpox vaccine was responsible for an increase in smallpox-related deaths, and was said, in England and Wales alone, to "kill 14,000 infants a year and probably injured 140,000 a year." Vaccinees also became more susceptible to diphtheria, tuberculosis, and cancer. [Levine, 58; Miller, 1996: 24-25; Miller, 1993: 45-46; Hale, 106, 113-114; Chase, 62.]

147. Both Henri Toussaint and Emil Roux were denied due credit for their work by Pasteur. The greatest breach of ethics occurred during the development of the anthrax vaccine. Toussaint had discovered an effective vaccine, but since many animals became ill after vaccination, he revised his methods. Although Pasteur had developed his own vaccine using very different methods, he "borrowed" Toussaint's revised method and set his assistant Roux to work to develop a similar vaccine. In May

1881, Pasteur was challenged to perform a public experiment using his own vaccine. Instead, Pasteur substituted Roux's vaccine and falsely claimed, in print, that it was his own vaccine. [Tizard, 12-13; Gillispie, 395.]

148. Edelson, 55. Serial passages through another species in order to attenuate a pathogen was discovered by Dr. Burden-Sanderson in 1878. [Tizard, 15.]

149. James, 87-88.

150. Dolan and Taylor, 29.

151. Appel, 1999, 311.

152. Arya, 1405.

153. Appel, 1999, 311.

154. Fekadu, 1991(a): 368.

155. Centers for Disease Control, 1989; Also see CDC, 1991; Also see CDC, 1999; National Advisory Committee on Immunization, 149; Plotkin and Koprowski, 654.

156. Botros et al., 137.

157. Fekadu, 1991(a): 369.

158. Homeopathic remedies for treating rabies miasm are listed in this book along with symptoms that will help the owner determine which remedies may be most effective. [Hamilton, 255.]

159. Pitcairn and Pitcairn, 325.

160. Ibid., 325-326.

161. Ibid.

162. Pedersen et al., 1978, 1092-1096. The following article describes cases of vaccine failure as well as suspected cases of vaccine-induced rabies. [Okoh.]

163. Pedersen et al., 1978, 1094.

164. Ibid., 1092,

165. This article also notes anaphylaxis in cattle following the use of inactivated rabies vaccine, and encephalitis in cattle following the use of rabies vaccines containing mouse brain extracts. [Wilcock and Yager, 1174.]

166. Kathy Goyeau, Groom at the Top, Professional Dog Grooming, Windsor, Ontario, consultation, December 20, 2001.

167. 25 TAC Sec.169.29; Ernest Oertli, Zoonosis Control Division Veterinarian, Texas Department of Health, Personal Communication, May 20, 2002.

168. Duval and Giger, 290-295.

169. Ibid., 294.

170. Dodds, 719, 729.

171. Ibid., 719.

172. Ibid., 291.

173. A "nonvaccine" control IMHA group was compared; mortality was 44% for this group. The mortality rates were not significantly different between the "vaccine" and "nonvaccine" groups, but it must also be understood that *all* dogs were vaccinated. The criteria for separating the two groups was simply that the interval between

vaccination and IMHA-onset fell within one month for the "vaccine" group and was between one month and 55 months for the "nonvaccine" group. [Ibid., 290.]

Feline

1. Retroviruses are RNA viruses that contain an enzyme called *reverse transcriptase* (RT). Under normal circumstances, "it is the DNA that directs the manufacture of all new proteins and other cell parts, including RNA." RT reverses this process. The viral RNA becomes integrated into the host's DNA, taking over the cell's reproductive machinery, where it manufactures more viruses, rather than healthy new cells. The resulting proviral DNA strand is not recognized by the immune system as foreign so the immune system will not respond. The virus can remain dormant for an indefinite period until it is reactivated. [Horowitz, 66; Diodati, 79-80.]

2. There are a variety of FeLV strains. They tend to mutate and recombine within the host, essentially creating new virus variants. FeLV-A is the most common and may become altered within the cat producing FeLV-B or FeLV-C. For more information regarding various strains, see: [Hoover and Mullins, 1290; Aiello, 555.]

3. *Viremia* means *the presence of virus in the blood*. While it is possible for the virus to remain latent in the cells of some cats with the regressive disease, the risk of reactivation of the virus is minimal. [Hoover and Mullins, 1288.]

4. Ibid.

5. Blood and Studdert, 441.

6. American Association of Feline Practitioners, 9.

7. Hoover and Mullins, 1288.

8. Rojko and Kociba, 1306-1307.

9. Ibid., 1307.

10. Pederson and Ott, 8.

11. Since there is a high spontaneous recovery rate for cats naturally infected with FeLV, the cats used in this experiment were artificially immunosuppressed with steroids.

12. Tizard and Bass, 1410.

13. Pederson and Ott, 14-15.

14. Ibid., 17-18.

15. Ibid., 8, 18.

16. A lively debate between Pederson, Ott and the vaccine developers followed the publication of this study. Interestingly enough, allegations lodged by Norden against Pederson and Ott did not dispute their findings about the vaccine's lack of efficacy. Instead, Norden claimed that the researchers had vested interests in discrediting Norden's vaccine; that data was altered; that the animals used in the experiments were exposed to FeLV before the time allotted for challenge-exposure; and that infected animals were not held long enough to see if they would recover. Pederson

and Ott addressed all of the allegations well. See: ["FeLV Vaccine Commentary," *Feline Practice* 16 no.1 (January-February 1986): 4-11; (May-June 1986): 5-8; (July-August 1986): 4-7.]

17. Pollock and Haffer, 1407. Citing efficacy reports on Haffer's 1987-1989 studies.

18. A subunit-recombinant vaccine utilizes two technologies that are becoming popular in contemporary vaccine development. Subunit vaccines use one part of the antigen (a surface glycoprotein of the virus, in this case) that should be capable of eliciting an immune response without causing the disease. Subunit vaccines, on their own, tend to elicit only weak immune responses. Recombinant vaccines insert the genetic material of one antigen (e.g. FeLV) into another antigen. In this case the FeLV glycoprotein was inserted into E. coli to strengthen the immune response to the subunit. Another vaccine of this type has been develeoped which uses the *Rous Sarcoma virus* (instead of the FeLV virus) inserted into feline herpesvirus type 1. Out of four vaccinates tested using this vaccine, three appeared to be protected from FeLV viremia, but the infectious virus was recovered from the bone marrow of all but one cat 12 weeks after challenge with the virus. For further information on this study, see: [Willemse et al., 1511-1516.]

19. Jarrett and Ganière, 9.

20. There are three subtypes of FeLV: FeLV-A, FeLV-B and FeLV-C. All FeLV isolates will contain FeLV-A, 50% also contain FeLV-B and approximately 2% contain FeLV-C. The second trial was of interest because this vaccine, unlike the inactivated vaccines, only contained the FeLV-A subtype. [Ibid., 7, 9.]

21. American Association of Feline Practitioners, 9.

22. Ibid.

23. Ibid.

24. Vaccine-induced fibrosarcomas will be discussed in more detail.

25. Neutrophils are white blood cells that are important to the initial immune response and to the destruction and removal of pathogens and cellular debris.

26. Blood and Studdert, 441.

27. Aiello, 586.

28. Blood and Studdert, 441.

29. Aiello, 586.

30. Levy, 285.

31. Ibid.

32. Certainly a queen that is experiencing clinical signs of immuno-suppression, with a significant reduction in $CD4^+$ cells, will pose a risk to her offspring, but otherwise there appears to be little risk to the fetus or nursling. Nurslings, in fact, will receive FIV-specific antibodies from their infected mother which will confer protection for several months. [Levy, 285.]

33. O'Connor et al., 1352.

34. Levy, 287.

35. For more information on HIV vaccine research, see: [Diodati, 228-

236.] Many FIV strains have been isolated throughout the world and have been categorized into four subtypes. They have been designated as subtypes, or clades, (A-D). Most FIV vaccine research has concentrated on subtypes A and B due to their prevalence. [Elyar et al., 1442.]

36. The vaccines used in this study include: FIV ISCOMs (immune stimulating complexes), recombinant (expressed in E. coli) FIV p24 ISCOMs, and a fixed, inactivated cell vaccine. [Hosie et al., 194.]

37. Huisman et al., 183-185. Similar results were found in the following study: [Verschoor et al., 285-289.] The latter study, however, did not detect viral enhancement following vaccination and challenge, but infrequent sampling may explain this.

38. Huisman et al., 186.

39. This vaccine used cells, derived from the test subjects themselves, that were freshly infected with the FIV virus. [Karlas et al., 358.]

40. By week two, vaccinated cats were found to have between 10-36 infected cells per million. This increased to 110-385/10^6 by week four. At week four, control cats had between 35-80/10^6 infected cells. From week five onward, the "differences in viral load became less clear." [Ibid.]

41. Hesselink et al., 110.

42. Matteucci et al., 122.

43. There are no apparent differences in the strains that would explain the difference in virulence between FECV and FIPV. [Addie et al., 24.]

44. The virus is also related to swine transmissible gastroenteritis virus (TGEV), canine coronavirus, and the respiratory corona virus of humans. Swine and canine coronaviruses can infect cats. Usually *subclinical* infections result but one canine coronavirus isolate has been known to cause clinical FIP in cats. The FECV (enteric coronavirus) replicates mainly in the intestines whereas the FIPV multiplies in the intestines and respiratory tract, then spreads through the body infecting macrophages and monocytes. [Vennema et al., 1998: 150-157; Canadian Animal Health Institute, 739; Scott, 349; Gerber et al., 536.]

45. Rohrbach et al., 1114.

46. In this study, Persian and Birman catteries were examined. It was found that, even when environmental factors were removed (e.g. proximity), cats with FIP-affected relatives were more susceptible than unrelated cats. The authors also noted a previous study where Abyssinian cats demonstrated "significantly longer survival times after challenge with virulent FIP strains than other breeds in their study." Susceptibility to FIP may depend, in part, on genetic factors. See also: [Foley and Pederson, 14-22.]

47. Uncertainty remains concerning the natural routes of transmission.

48. Scott, 349.

49. Hoskins, 14.

50. American Association of Feline Practitioners, 9.

51. Aiello, 552.

52. Treatment is generally aimed at alleviating signs. Only about 1/3 of cats with mild signs will respond favorably, i.e. experience a short-term remission, but none of the current treatments are considered to be

curative. [Evermann et al., 1133; Hoskins, 9-10.]

53. Approximately ¾ of clinical cases are effusive. [Fehr et al., 1101; Evermann et al., 1130.]

54. Aiello, 552.

55. Ibid., 553-554.

56. Evermann et al., 1130.

57. Wolf, Alice M., 28. See also, Addie and Jarrett, 133.

58. Other studies have found no difference in outcome for vaccinated versus unvaccinated cats. [Scott, 353.]

59. Fehr et al., 1106-1107.

60. Olsen, 23.

61. The following study applies this principle to parenteral vaccines used prior to the temperature-sensitive intranasal vaccine. This vaccine apparently allows the virus to grow at temperatures found in the nasopharynx (31°C) but not at systemic sites where the temperature is higher (39°C). The authors claim that the intranasal vaccine does elicit both a humoral and cellular immune response. However, they could not make any substantial efficacy claims due to the study's design. Cats were not exposed to coronavirus experimentally, and there is no mention of the disease's prevalence in the field during the study period, so neither the vaccine's efficacy, nor its potential to sensitize the cats, was actually determined. [Reeves et al., 117, 120.] In contrast, the following study did challenge vaccinated and unvaccinated cats. It found the vaccine to be effective in most cats and noted that it did not cause ADE. [Gerber et al., 538.]

62. Scott, 351; Pedersen and Boyle, 868. See also, Venemma et al., 1990: 1407; Pederson and Black, 229.

63. Circulating antibody enhances the infection of macrophages. ADE has also been noted in the experimental infection of animals but it is unclear whether this occurs with natural infection. [Gerber et al., 536; Scott, 351.]

64. Scott, 352.

65. Compare with Wolf, Alice M., 28.

66. Feline calicivirus has not been known to cause the serious haemorrhagic disease in cats that calicivirus causes in rabbits. However, a recent report described a calicivirus-caused haemorrhagic disease in six cats. The antigen, called FCV-Ari, is genetically similar to the less pathogenic calicivirus field strains. Mortality from this strain is estimated at 33-50%. Vaccination appeared to provide *some* protection to some cats against severe manifestations but it did not prevent infection, and all of the cats who died during this study were vaccinated. See also: [Pederson et al, 2000: 281-300.]

67. Yokoyama et al., 1657.

68. FCV can be shed continuously for months while FVR can be shed intermittently for months. The intermittent FVR shedding appears to be associated with stress. [Aiello, 1115.]

69. The role of the chronic carrier state in pregnancy and birth is uncertain. Some kittens may be infected at birth and become quite ill

quickly or they may suffer only a mild case due to the protection of maternal antibodies. Others may never develop signs but the exposure will confer permanent immunity. See also: [Wardley, 338.]

70. Aiello, 1115.

71. A recombinant FHV/FCV vaccine has been under development. [Yokoyama et al., 1657-1663.]

72. Scott and Geissinger, 652.

73. Wardley, 338.

74. Radford et al., 117.

75. Provocation disease has been reported after many different vaccines. Almroth Wright, inventor of the typhoid vaccine, first discovered this phenomenon in 1901. For more information, see: [Diodati, 80.]

76. Wardley, 338.

77. In this case, the intranasal vaccine was studied, but viral shedding is *not* limited to this vaccine-type only. [Orr and Gaskell, 164-165.]

78. The vaccines studied were *Felocell CVR-C* and *Eclipse 4*. Short-term reactions included: lethargy, inappetence, or occasional pain which developed 4-12 hours post- vaccination and resolved within 36 hours. [Starr, 316-317.]

79. The author of the study theorized that delayed reactions were largely related to the Chlamydia portion of the combination vaccine since delayed reactions were rarely reported to the manufacturer when vaccines without Chlamydia were used. This is an interesting observation in that he also said that delayed reactions, in general, had never been reported in the literature before this study. [Ibid., 320, 322.]

80. Scott and Geissinger, 652.

81. See also, American Association of Feline Practitioners, 8.

82. Canadian Animal Health Institute, 525.

83. Hoskins et al., 12.

84. American Association of Feline Practitioners, 10. Intervet's *PROTEX-Bb* Product Information Sheet states that kittens vaccinated at four weeks of age "were protected against disease when challenged three weeks post-vaccination" and that onset of immunity occurred 72 hours post-vaccination in eight-week-old kittens. See also: [http://www.protexbb.com/breeders/bb_frame.html]

85. American Association of Feline Practitioners, 10-11.

86. See also, Sturgess et al., 668.

87. Aiello, 1116.

88. American Association of Feline Practitioners, 9.

89. Sturgess et al., 668-669.

90. American Association of Feline Practitioners, 9.

91. In 1947, a feline panleukopenia-enteritis-like disease appeared on mink farms. The outbreaks began in Canada but spread rapidly to mink farms throughout the world. The virus was found to be serologically indistinguishable from feline panleukopenia virus. How this feline disease entered the mink population is unknown but may have been the result of a mutation or variation that allowed the virus to expand its host range. It is important to note, however, that ferrets, who share the Mustelidae

family classification with mink, have been infected with the feline panleukopenia virus under experimental conditions, so an expansion of the viral host range seems plausible in this case. [Siegl, 368.]

92. Aiello, 559.

93. American Association of Feline Practitioners, 5; Scott and Geissinger, 652.

94. Ibid.

95. Kits vaccinated at three days old did not show signs of neurological damage and appeared to be normal. [Duenwald et al., 395-396.]

96. Ibid. This is based upon CPV-2 vaccine studies in puppies. Similar studies have not been performed on cats.

97. Bunn, 383.

98. Ibid.

99. Rupprecht and Childs, 15, 19.

100. Bunn, 385-386.

101. Esh and Cunningham, 1338.

102. Bunn, 382.

103. In this case, it was the ERA-strain MLV vaccine, produced by Jensen-Salsbery Laboratories, that was given to each of the cats. The manufacturer later withdrew this vaccine for use in cats. This article also describes a fifth cat that contracted rabies from a different live rabies vaccine. [Esh and Cunningham, 1336-9.]

104. Ibid., 1337.

105. Bunn, 385.

106. Hendrick et al., 1992, 5391-5394.

107. Ibid., 5391. "Macrophages," or large "cell-eaters," are the immune system's first line of defense. When presented with something identified by the body as "foreign," macrophages will envelop and digest the foreign material, bring identifiers to their surfaces, and cause other immune cells to mature and elicit an immune defense.

108. Ibid., 5394.

109. Esplin et al., 1993, 1246.

110. Similar reactions were noted following imtramuscular rabies vaccination, sub-cutaneous distemper vaccination, and subcutaneous feline viral rhinotracheitis, calici and panleukopenia (FVRCP) vaccination. [Hendrick and Dunagan, 304-305.]

111. American Assoc. of Feline Practitioners and Academy of Feline Medicine's Advisory Panel. http://www.api4animals.org/doc.asp?ID=556

112. DeBoer et al.

113. Macy, "Feline Vaccination Schedules..."

114. Many types of vaccine-site sarcomas have been described including: fibrosarcomas, osteosarcomas, rhabdomyosarcomas, malignant histiocytomas, and chondrosarcomas.

115. A veterinarian reported vaccine-site sarcoma development in two cats under his care, eight and eleven years following rabies and FeLV vaccinations, respectively. [Murray, 955.]

116. Macy and Hendrick, 103-104.

117. Ibid., 104.

118. Some measure of inflammation will occur frequently following vaccination but this does not necessarily indicate tumor development.

119. It has been noted, for example, that chickens will develop aggressive metastasizing tumors when infected with the Rous sarcoma virus *unless* "postwounding inflammation can be suppressed." [Macy and Hendrick, 105.]

120. The vaccine antigen (virus, in this case) may be culpable as well.

121. Esplin et al., 1993: 1245-1247.

122. Ibid., 1245.

123. Ibid.

124. Hendrick et al., 5391.

125. Kass et al., 396-405.

126. Ibid., 402.

127. Ibid., 400.

128. *Metastasis* refers to the spreading of the tumor cells to distant areas, usually via the bloodstream. [Ibid., 403.]

129. Esplin et al., 1996: 20-23; Sandler et al., 374.

130. Esplin et al., 1996: 24.

131. Lester et al., 91-95.

132. Ibid., 92-93.

133. Ibid., 92.

134. Ibid., 94.

135. Ibid., 92, 95.

136. The role of vaccine adjuvants in tumor development must be addressed. Reasons for guarding vaccine components as "proprietary" data cannot be supported. It is unethical to allow vaccine manufacturers such competitive secrecy when their products cause devastating effects. Any research in this area will be continually frustrated, and subject to undue repetition and expense, because researchers cannot access enough information to provide adequate conclusions. Veterinarians and researchers can hardly be expected to properly advise their clients if they are kept ignorant of vaccine components and their risks.

Holistic Pet Care Options

1. American Academy of Veterinary Acupuncture.
2. Hamilton, 387.
3. Dr. Susan Beal, personal communication, August 10, 2001.
4. Ibid.

Ethical and Legal Considerations

1. See, for example, Mullan and Boswall, 348. In this case, the judge determined that, even though there was only a small percentage (1/10th of 1%) of unexplained breast implant ruptures, this did not exonerate the manufacturer from providing adequate warnings.
2. Meisel and Kuczewski, 2521-2526.

3. Ibid.

4. Geyer, 1034.

5. Ibid., 1035.

6. Canadian Food Inspection Agency.

7. "**Type 1 reactions** [are] defined as any systemic adverse reaction, anaphylactic or hypersensitivity, requiring veterinary treatment including: persistent fever (lasting more than 48 hours), recumbency, persisting lethargy, decrease in activity, muscle tremors, shivering, hypersalivation, dyspnea and other respiratory problems, cyanosis, diarrhea, vomiting, colic and other gastrointestinal problems, significant persistent drop in production, abortions and other reproductive problems, neurological signs. **Type 2 reactions** [are] defined as death or an increase in mortality rate following vaccination. **Type 3 reactions** [are] defined as local persistent reactions (such as edema, abcess, granuloma, fibrosis, alopecia, hyper pigmentation) and/or excessive pain at injection site reported by a veterinarian or owner." [Ibid.]

8. The *Health of Animals Regulation, Part XI, 135.1*, states that "Every holder of a license or permit shall report to the Minister, in writing, any information concerning or any evidence of, a significant deficiency in safety, potency or efficacy of a veterinary biologic within 15 days from the date on which such information or evidence is known to him or is generally known to the industry, whichever is earlier." SOR/79-839, s.32

9. Gumley, 27.

10. Ibid., 26.

11. Adverse events can be reported either online (http://www.usp.org), by telephone (1-800-487-7776), Fax (301-816-8532), or mail. The adverse event reporting form is available at: http://www.usp.org/frameset.htm? http://www.usp.org/prn/

12. Gumley, 27.

13. Meyer.

14. Ibid.

15. Dukelow and Nuse, 301-302.

16. Geyer, 1027, 1033-1034.

17. Ibid, 1038.

18. Jack, August 1997: 512.

19. Geyer, 1033. Citing *Ruden v. Hansen*, N. W. 2d 713 (Ia. 1973).

20. Geyer, 1028.

21. Jack, October 1997: 654; Geyer, 1042.

22. Geyer, 1042.

23. Jack, October 1997: 654.

24. Geyer, 1044.

25. A substitute may be required, for example, if the injured animal regularly appeared on a television program.

26. Geyer, 1042.

27. Macy, "Has the Time Come...?"

28. Geyer, 1048.

29. Macy, "Has the Time Come...?"

30. Geyer, 1048.

Bibliography

Addie, D. D. and O. Jarrett. "A Study of Naturally Occurring Feline Coronavirus Infections in Kittens," *Veterinary Record.* 130 no. 7 (February 15, 1992): 133-137.

Addie, D. D., S. Toth, G. D. Murray and O. Jarrett. "The Risk of Typical and Antibody Enhanced Feline Infectious Peritonitis Among Cats from Feline Coronavirus Endemic Households," *Feline Practice.* 23 no.3 (May/June 1995): 24-26.

Aiello, Susan E., ed. *The Merck Veterinary Manual.* 8th ed., Whitehouse Station, NJ: Merck & Co., Inc., 1998.

American Academy of Veterinary Acupuncture. Organizational pamphlet. http://www.aava.org

American Animal Hospital Association, "AAHA's Opinion Paper on Vaccine Issues." http://www.aahanet.org/web/position_state2.html

American Association of Feline Practitioners. *2000 Report of the American Association of Feline Practitioners and the Academy of Feline Medicine Advisory Panel on Feline Vaccines.* Nashville: American Association of Feline Practitioners, 2000.

American Veterinary Medical Association, "Compendium of Animal Rabies Prevention and Control, 2000." http://www.avma.org/pubhlth/rabcont.html

Anderson, Kenneth N., Lois E. Anderson and Walter D. Glanze. *Mosby's Medical, Nursing, and Allied Health.* St Louis, MO: Mosby-Year Book, Inc., 1994.

Anonymous. "Laboratory Accused of Spreading Virus While Working on Vaccine," *Western Daily Press,* (April 8, 2001).

Appel, M. J. G. "Lyme Disease in Dogs and Cats," *Compendium on Continuing Education for the Practicing Veterinarian.* 12 no.5 (May 1990): 617-626.

Appel, M. J. G. "Forty Years of Canine Vaccination," In *Advances in Veterinary Medicine.* Vol. 41., ed. Ron D. Schultz, 309-324. San Diego: Academic Press, 1999.

Appel, M. J. G. "Lyme Disease Vaccination," In *Kirk's Veterinary Therapy XIII: Small Animal Practice.* ed. John D. Bonagura, 256-258. Philadelphia: W. B. Saunders Company, 2000.

Appel, M. J. G. and J. H. Gillespie. "Canine Distemper Virus," in *Virology Monographs.* vol. 11, ed. S. Gard et al., (Wein: Springer-Verlag, 1972), 1-96.

Arya, Subhash C. "Blood Donated After Vaccination with Rabies Vaccine Derived from Sheep Brain Cells Might Transmit CJD," *British Medical Journal* 313 no.7069 (30 November 1996): 1405.

Baer, George M., ed. *The Natural History of Rabies.* 2nd. Ed. Boca Raton: CRC Press, 1991.

Bárcena, Juan, Mónica Morales, Belén Vázquez, José A. Boga, Francisco Parra, Javier Lucientes, Albert Pagès-Manté, José M. Sánchez-Vizcaíno, Rafael Blasco and Juan M. Torres. "Horizontal Transmissible Protection Against Myxomatosis and Rabbit Haemorrhagic Disease by

Using a Recombinant Myxoma Virus," *Journal of Virology*. 74 no.3 (February 2000): 1114-1123.

Bass, E. P., M. A. Gill and W. H. Beckenhauer. "Development of a Modified Live, Canine Origin Parvovirus Vaccine," *Journal of the American Veterinary Medical Association*. 181 no.9 (November 1, 1982): 909-913.

Bemis, D. A., H. A. Greisen and M. J. Appel. "Pathogenesis of Canine Bordellosis," *Journal of Infectious Diseases* 135 no.5 (May 1977): 753-762.

Bemis, David A., Max J. G. Appel. "Aerosol, Parenteral, and Oral Antibiotic Treatment of Bordetella Bronchiseptica Infections in Dogs," *Journal of the American Veterinary Medical Association*. 170 no.10 (May 15, 1977): 1082-1086.

Berns, Kenneth I., ed. *The Parvoviruses*. New York: Plenum Press, 1984.

Blixenkrone-Moller, M., V. Svansson, P. Have, C. Orvell, M. Appel, I. R. Pederson, H. H. Dietz and P. Henriksen. "Studies on Manifestations of Canine Distemper Virus Infection in an Urban Dog Population," *Veterinary Microbiology*. 37 no.1-2 (October 1993): 163-173.

Blood, D. C. and V. P. Studdert. *Saunders Comprehensive Veterinary Dictionary*. 2nd ed., London: WB Saunders, 1999.

Botros, B. A. M., J. C. Lewis and M. Kerkor. "A Study to Evaluate Non-Fatal Rabies in Animals," *Journal of Tropical Medicine and Hygiene*. 82 no.7 (July 1979): 137-140.

Broughton, E. S. and J. Scarnell. "Prevention of Renal Carriage of Leptospirosis in Dogs by Vaccination," *The Veterinary Record*. 117 no.12 (September 21, 1985): 307-311.

Brown, F. "Review of Accidents Caused by Incomplete Inactivation of Viruses," *Developments in Biological Standardization*. 81 (1993): 103-107.

Brunner, Cindy J. and Larry J. Swango. "Canine Parvovirus Infection: Effects on the Immune System and Factors that Predispose to Severe Disease," *The Compendium of Continuing Education*. 7 no.12 (December 1985): 979-989.

Bunn, Thomas O. "Cat Rabies," *The Natural History of Rabies* 2nd ed. ed George M. Baer, 379-387. Boca Raton: CRC Press, 1991.

Buttram, Harold E. and John Chriss Hoffman. *Vaccinations and Immune Malfunction*. Quakertown, PA: The Humanitarian Publishing Co., 1985.

Canadian Animal Health Institute. *Compendium of Veterinary Products*. 6th ed. Hensall, ON: North American Compendiums Ltd., 1999.

Canadian Food Inspection Agency, Veterinary Biologics and Biotechnology Section. "Guidelines for Reporting Suspected Adverse Reactions to Veterinary Biologics," (February 24, 1998): http://www.cfia-acia.agr.ca/english/anima/vetbio/vb315e.shtml

Carmichael, L. E. "Part 2: Vaccines for Dogs," In *Veterinary Vaccinology*. ed. P. P. Pastoret, J. Blancou, P. Vannier and C. Verschueren, 326-335. Amsterdam: Elsevier, 1997.

Carmichael, L. E. "Canine Viral Vaccines at a Turning Point— A Personal Perspective," In *Advances in Veterinary Medicine*. Vol. 41., ed. Ronald D. Schultz, 289-308. San Diego: Academic Press, 1999.

Carmichael, L. E., J. C. Joubert and R. V. H. Pollock. "A Modified

Live Canine Parvovirus Strain with Novel Plaque Characteristics. I. Viral Attenuation and Dog Response," *Cornell Vet.* 71 no.3 (1981): 408-427.

Centers for Disease Control and Prevention. "Summary of Notifiable Diseases, United States, 1989," *Morbidity and Mortality Weekly Report.* 38 no.54 (1989).

Centers for Disease Control and Prevention. "Summary of Notifiable Diseases, United States, 1991," *Morbidity and Mortality Weekly Report.* 40 no.53 (1991).

Centers for Disease Control and Prevention. "Mass Treatment of Humans Exposed to Rabies – New Hampshire, 1994," *Morbidity and Mortality Weekly Report.* 44 no.26 (July 7, 1995): 484-486.

Centers for Disease Control and Prevention. "Summary of Notifiable Diseases, United States, 1999," *Morbidity and Mortality Weekly Report.* 47 no.53 (1999).

Chalmers, W. S. and W. Baxendale. "A Comparison of Canine Distemper Vaccine and Measles Vaccine for the Prevention of Canine Distemper in Young Puppies," *The Veterinary Record.* 135 no.15 (October 8, 1994): 349-353.

Chase, Allan. *Magic Shots: A Human and Scientific Account of the Long and Continuing Struggle to Eradicate Infectious Diseases by Vaccination.* NY: William Morrow & Co., 1982.

Chladek, Dan W., James M. Williams, Don L. Gerber, Louis L. Harris and Fred M. Murdock. "Canine Parainfluenza-Bordetella Bronchiseptica Vaccine: Immunogenicity," *American Journal of Veterinary Research.* 42 no.2 (February 1981): 266-270.

DeBoer, D. J., K. A. Moriella, J. L. Blum, L. M. Volk and L. K. Bredahl. "Safety and Immunologic Effects After Inoculation of Inactivated and Combined Live-Inactivated Dermatophytosis Vaccines in Cats," *American Journal of Veterinary Research.* 63 no. 11 (November 2002): 1532-1537.

Diesch, Stanley L. "Leptospirosis: Vaccination and Titer Evaluation," *Modern Veterinary Practice.* 61 no.1 (November 1980): 905-908.

Diodati, Catherine J. M. *Immunization: History, Ethics, Law and Health.* Windsor, ON: Integral Aspects Inc., 1999.

Dodds, W. Jean. "More Bumps on the Vaccine Road," In *Advances in Veterinary Medicine.* Vol.41., ed. Ronald D. Schultz, 715-732. San Diego: Academic Press, 1999.

Dolan, T. M. and C. B. Taylor. "Is Pasteurism a Fraud?" *The Review of Reviews.* Vol. 2 (July-December 1890): 29.

DuChateau, Brian K., Douglas M. England, Steven M. Callister, Lony C.L. Lim, Steven D. Lovrich and Ronald F. Schell. "Macrophages Exposed to Borrelia Burgdorferi Induce Lyme Arthritis in Hamsters," *Infection and Immunity.* 64 no.7 (July 1996): 2540-2547.

Duenwald, J. C., J. M. Holland, J. R. Gorham and R. L. Orr. "Feline Panleukopenia: Experimental Cerebellar Hypoplasia Produced in Neonatal Ferrets with Live Virus Vaccine," *Research in Veterinary Science.* 12 no. 4-6 (1971): 394-396.

Dukelow, Daphne A. and Betsy Nuse. *Pocket Dictionary of Canadian Law.* Scarborough, ON: Thompson Professional Publishing, 1995.

Dunbar, Bonnie. "Hepatitis B Vaccine," http://www.ias.org.nz/dunbar.htm.

Dunn, Tom, Sarah K. Abood, Don Polley, Johnny D. Hoskins and Michael D. Willard. "Clinical Management of Canine Parvovirus, Part 1," *Canine Practice.* 20 no.5 (September/October 1995): 10-14.

Dunn, Tom, Sarah K. Abood, Don Polley, Johnny D. Hoskins and Michael D. Willard. "Clinical Management of Canine Parvovirus, Part 2," *Canine Practice.* 20 no.6 (November/December 1995): 11-16.

Duval, Derek and Urs Giger. "Vaccine-Associated Immune-Mediated Hemolytic Anemia in the Dog," *Journal of Veterinary Internal Medicine.* 10 no.5 (September-October 1996): 290-295.

Edelson, Edward. *The Immune System.* NY: Chelsea Publishing House, 1989.

Ek-Kommomen, C., L. Sihvonen, K. Pekkanen, U. Rikula and L. Nuotio. "Outbreak of Canine Distemper in Vaccinated Dogs in Finland," *The Veterinary Record.* 141 no. 15 (October 11, 1997): 380-383.

Elyar, John S., Marinka C. Tellier, Jeanne M. Soos and Janet K. Yamamoto. "Perspectives on FIV Vaccine Development," *Vaccine.* 15 no.12-13 (1997): 1437-1444.

EPA, "Emergency First Aid Treatment Guide for Propiolactone, Beta," http://www.epa.gov/ swercepp/ehs/firstaid/57578.txt

Esh, James B. and James G. Cunningham. "Vaccine Induced Rabies in Four Cats," *Journal of the American Veterinary Medical Association.* 180 no.11 (June 1, 1982):1336-1339.

Esplin, D. Glen, L. D. McGill, Anne C. Meininger and Sharon R. Wilson. "Postvaccination Sarcomas in Cats," *Journal of the American Veterinary Medical Association.* 202 no.8 (April 15, 1993): 1245-1247.

Esplin, D. Glen, Michael H. Jaffe and L. D. McGill. "Metastasizing Liposarcoma Associated With a Vaccination Site in a Cat," *Feline Practice.* 24 no.5 (Sept/Oct 1996): 20-23.

Essex, Max and Phyllis J. Kanki. "The Origins of the AIDS Virus," *Scientific American.* 259 no.4 (October 1988): 64-71.

Evermann, James F., Carolyn J. Henry and Steven L. Marks. "Feline Infectious Peritonitis," *Journal of the American Veterinary Medical Association.* 206 no.8 (April 15, 1995): 1130-1134.

Fehr, Daniela, Edgar Holznagel, Stefania Bolla, Beat Hauser, Arnold A. P. M. Herrewegh, Marian C. Horzinek and Hans Lutz. "Placebo-Controlled Evaluation of a Modified Live Virus Vaccine Against Feline Infectious Peritonitis: Safety and Efficacy Under Field Conditions," *Vaccine.* 15 no.10 (1997): 1101-1109.

Fekadu, Makonnen. "Canine Rabies," *The Natural History of Rabies.* 2nd ed. ed George M. Baer, 367-378. Boca Raton: CRC Press, 1991(a).

Fekadu, Makonnen. "Latency and Aborted Rabies," *The Natural History of Rabies.* 2nd ed. ed George M. Baer, 191-198. Boca Raton: CRC Press, 1991(b).

Fishman, B. and J. Scarnell. "Persistence of Protection After Vaccination Against Infectious Canine Hepatitis Virus (CAV/1)," *The Veterinary Record.* (December 18 and 25, 1976): 509.

Foley, Janet E. and Neils C. Pederson. "The Inheritance of Susceptibility to Feline Infectious Peritonitis in Purebred Catteries," *Feline Practice.* 24 no.1 (Jan/Feb 1996): 14-22.

Gerber, J. D., J. D. Ingersol!, A. M. Gast, K. K. Christianson, N. L. Selzer, R. M. Landon, N. E. Pfeiffer, R. L. Sharpee and W. H. Beckenhauer. "Protection Against Feline Infectious Peritonitis by Intranasal Inoculation of a Temperature-Sensitive FIPV Vaccine," *Vaccine.* 8 (1990): 536-542.

Geyer, L. Leon. "Malpractice and Liability," *Veterinary Clinics of North America: Small Animal Practice.* 23 no.5 (September 1993): 1027-1052.

Gillispie, Charles C., ed. *Dictionary of Science Biography* Vol. X. NY: Charles Scribner's Sons, 1974.

Goldstein, Martin. *The Nature of Animal Healing.* NY: Alfred A. Knopf, 1999.

Gooding, G. E. and W. F. Robinson. "Maternal Antibody, Vaccination and Reproductive Failure in Dogs with Parvovirus Infection," *Australian Veterinary Journal.* 59 no.6 (December 1982): 170-174.

Goodnow, R. A. and F. J. Shade. "Industry Reports: Control of Canine Bordetellosis," *Modern Veterinary Practice.* (July 1980): 597-598.

Green, Sherril L. "Rabies," *Veterinary Clinics of North America: Equine Practice.* 13 no.1 (April 1997): 1-11.

Gumley, Nigel. "Revaccination Guidelines Revisited," *Canadian Veterinary Journal.* 41 no.1 (January 2000): 27.

Hale, Annie Riley. *The Medical Voodoo.* NY: Gotham House, 1935.

Hamilton, Don. *Homeopathic Care for Cats and Dogs.* Berkeley, CA: North Atlantic Books, 1999.

Hendrick, Mattie J. and Corrine A. Dunagan. "Focal Necrotizing Granulomatous Panniculitis Associated with Subcutaneous Injection of Rabies Vaccine in Cats and Dogs: 10 Cases (1988-1989)," *Journal of the American Veterinary Medical Association.* 198 no.2 (January 15, 1991): 304-305.

Hendrick, Mattie J., Michael H. Goldschmidt, Frances S. Shofer, Yun-Yu Wang and Andrew P. Somlyo. "Postvaccinal Sarcomas in the Cat: Epidemiology and Electron Probe Microanalytical Identification of Aluminum," *Cancer Research.* 52 (October 1, 1992): 5391-5394.

Hesselink, W. O. Sondermeijer, H. Pouwels, E. Verblakt and C. Dhore. "Vaccination of Cats Against Feline Immunodeficiency Virus (FIV): A Matter of Challenge," *Veterinary Microbiology.* 69 no.1-2 (1999): 109-110.

Hilleman, Maurice R. "Six Decades of Vaccine Development—A Personal History," *Nature Medicine.* 4 no. 5 Supplement (May 1998): 507-514.

Hoover, Edward A. and James I. Mullins. "Feline Leukemia Virus Infection and Diseases," *Journal of the American Veterinary Medical Association.* 199 no.10 (November 15, 1991): 1287-1297.

Hoover, John P., Charles A. Baldwin and Charles E. Rupprecht. "Serologic Response of Domestic Ferrets (Mustela Putorius Furo) to Canine Distemper and Rabies Virus Vaccines," *Journal of the American Veterinary Medical Association.* 194 no.2 (January 15, 1989): 234-238.

Horowitz, Leonard G. *Emerging Viruses: AIDS & Ebola: Nature, Accident or Intentional?* Rockport, MA: Tetrahedron, Inc., 1997.

Horzinek, Marian C. "Vaccination: A Philosophical View," In *Advances in Veterinary Medicine.* Vol. 41., ed. Ronald D. Schultz, 1-6. San Diego:

Academic Press, 1999.

Hosie, Margaret J., Robert Osborne, George Reid, James C. Neil and Oswald Jarrett. "Enhancement After Feline Immunodeficiency Virus Vaccination," *Veterinary Immunology and Immunopathology.* 35 no.1-2 (1992) 191-197.

Hoskins, Johnny D. "Coronavirus Infection in Cats," *Veterinary Clinics of North America: Small Animal Practice.* 23 no.1 (January 1993): 1-16.

Hoskins, Johnny, James Richards, Elaine M. Rayne, Grant Gugisberg, Karen Duncan, Mike Lappin and Bill Fortney. "Feline Bordetella Bronchiseptica: Part 1," *Feline Practice.* 27 no.3 (May/June 1999): 10-12.

Huisman, Willem, Jos A. Karlas, Kees H. J. Seibelink, Robin C. Huisman, Anthony de Ronde, Michael J. Francis, Guus F. Rimmelzwaan and Albert D. M. E. Osterhaus. "Feline Immunodeficiency Virus Subunit Vaccines that Induce Virus Neutralising Antibodies but No Protection Against Challenge Infection," *Vaccine.* 16 no.2-3 (1998): 181-187.

Jack, Douglas C. "The Legal Implications of the Veterinarians Role as a Private Practitioner and Health Professional, with Particular Reference to the Human-Animal Bond: Part 1, The Law of Negligence," *Canadian Veterinary Journal.* 38 no.8 (August 1997): 511-516.

Jack, Douglas C. "The Legal Implications of the Veterinarians Role as a Private Practitioner and Health Professional, with Particular Reference to the Human-Animal Bond: Part 2, The Veterinarians Role in Society," *Canadian Veterinary Journal.* 38 no.10 (October 1997): 653-659.

Jacobson, Richard H., Yung-Fu Chang and Sang J. Shin. "Lyme Disease: Laboratory Diagnosis of Infected and Vaccinated Symptomatic Dogs," *Seminars in Veterinary Medicine and Surgery (Small Animal).* 11 no.3 (August 1996): 172-182.

James, Walene. *Immunization: The Reality Behind the Myth.* Westport, CT: Bergin & Garvey, 1995.

Jarrett, O. and J.-P. Ganière. "Comparative Studies of the Efficacy of a Recombinant Feline Leukemia Virus Vaccine," *The Veterinary Record.* (January 6, 1996): 7-10.

Johnson, F. Brent. "Parvovirus Proteins," In *The Parvoviruses.* ed. Kenneth I. Berns, 259-295. New York: Plenum Press, 1984.

Karlas, Jos A., Kees H. J. Siebelink, Maartje A. v. Peer, Willem Huisman, Guus F. Rimmelzwaan and Albert D. M. E. Osterhaus. "Accelerated Viraemia in Cats Vaccinated with Fixed Autologous FIV-Infected Cells," *Veterinary Immunology and Immunopathology.* 65 no.2-4 (1998): 353-365.

Karzon, D. T. "Measles Virus," *Annals of the New York Academy of Sciences.* 101 (1962): 527-539.

Kass, Philip H., William G. Barnes Jr., W. L. Spangler, Bruno B. Chomel and M. R. Culbertson. "Epidemiologic Evidence for a Causal Relation Between Vaccination and Fibrosarcoma Tumorigenesis in Cats," *Journal of the American Veterinary Medical Association.* 203 no.3 (August 1, 1993): 396-405.

Kontor, E. J., R. J. Wegrzyn and R. A. Goodnow. "Canine Infectious Tracheobronchitis: Effects of an Intranasal Live Canine Parainfluenza-

Bordetella Bronchiseptica Vaccine on Viral Shedding and Clinical Tracheobronchitis (Kennel Cough)," *American Journal of Veterinary Research.* 42 no.10 (October 1981): 1694-1698.

Krakowka, Steven, Richard G. Olsen, Michael K. Axthelm, Jacqueline Rice and Karen Winters. "Canine Parvovirus Infection Potentiates Canine Distemper Encephalitis Attributable to Modified Live-Virus Vaccine," *Journal of the American Veterinary Medical Association.* 180 (January 15, 1982): 137-9.

Krebs, John W., Jean S. Smith, Charles E. Rupprecht and James E. Childs. "Rabies Surveillance in the United States During 1998," *Journal of the American Veterinary Medical Association.* 215 no.12 (1999): 1786-1798.

Krebs, John W., Charles E. Rupprecht and James E. Childs. "Rabies Surveillance in the United States During 1999," *Journal of the American Veterinary Medical Association.* 217 no. 12 (2000): 1799-1811.

Kruth, Stephen A. and John A. Ellis. "Vaccination of Dogs and Cats: General Principles and Duration of Immunity," *Canadian Veterinary Journal.* 39 no.7 (July 1998): 423-426.

Larson, L. J. and R. D. Schultz. "Comparison of Selected Canine Vaccines for Their Ability to Induce Protective Immunity Against Canine Parvovirus Infection," *American Journal of Veterinary Research.* 58 no.4 (April 1997): 360-363.

Lester, Sally, Terri Clemett and Alf Burt. "Vaccine Site-Associated Sarcomas in Cats: Clinical Experience and a Laboratory Review (1982-1993)," *Journal of the American Animal Hospital.* 32 no.2 (March-April 1996): 91-95.

Levine, Arnold J. *Viruses.* NY: Scientific American Library, 1992.

Levy, Julie K. "CVT Update: Feline Immunodeficiency Virus," In *Kirk's Veterinary Therapy XIII: Small Animal Practice.* ed. John D. Bonagura, 284-288. Philadelphia: W. B. Saunders Company, 2000.

Lim, Lony C. L., Douglas M. England, Brian K. DuChateau, Nicole J. Glowacki and Ronald F. Schell. "Borrelia Burgdorferi-Specific T Lymphocytes Induce Severe Destructive Lyme Arthritis," *Infection and Immunity.* 63 no.4 (April 1995): 1400-1408.

Livini, Ephrat. "Vaccine Victims? The Controversy Surrounding SmithKline Beecham's LYMErix," abcNEWS.com (May 17, 2000)

Ma, Jianneng, Paul M. Hine, Ellen R. Clough, Durland Fish, Richard T. Coughlin, Gerald A. Beltz and Marvin G. Shew. "Safety, Efficacy and Immunogenicity of a Recombinant Osp Subunit Canine Lyme Disease Vaccine," *Vaccine.* 14 no.14 (1996): 1366-1374.

Macy, Dennis W. "Feline Vaccination Schedules: Another Look," http://www.geocities.com/~kremersark/macy699.html

Macy, Dennis W. "Has the Time Come for a Veterinary Vaccine Injury Act?" http://www.passport.ca/~bstanley/macy1.htm

Macy, Dennis W. and Mattie J. Hendrick. "The Potential Role of Inflammation in the Development of Postvaccinal Sarcomas in Cats," *Veterinary Clinics of North America: Small Animal Practice.* 26 no.1 (January 1996): 103-109.

Martin, Mary Louise. "Canine Coronavirus Enteritis and a Recent Outbreak

Following Modified Live Virus Vaccination," *Compendium on Continuing Education for the Practicing Veterinarian.* 7 no.12 (December 1985): 1012-1017.

Matteucci, Donatella, Mauro Pistello, Paola Mazzetti, Simone Gianecchini, Patrizia Isola, Antonio Merico, Lucia Zaccaro, Angela Rizzuti and Mauro Bendinelli. "AIDS Vaccination Studies Using Feline Immunodeficiency Virus as a Model: Immunisation with Inactivated Whole Virus Suppresses Viraemia Levels Following Intravaginal Challenge with Infected Cells but Not Following Intravenous Challenge with Cell-Free Virus," *Vaccine.* 18 no.1-2 (2000): 119-130.

McCandlish, I. A. P., H. Thompson and N. G. Wright. "Kennel Cough: Vaccination Against Bordetella Bronchiseptica Infection," *Veterinary Record.* 98 no.8 (February 21, 1976): 156-157.

McCandlish, I. A. P., H. Thompson and N. G. Wright. "Vaccination Against Canine Bordetellosis Using an Aluminum Hydroxide Adjuvant Vaccine," *Research in Veterinary Science.* 25 no.1 (July 1978): 51-57.

McCandlish, I. A. P., H. J. C. Cornwell, H. Thompson, A. S. Nash and C. M. Lowe. "Distemper Excephalitis in Pups After Vaccination of the Dam," *The Veterinary Record.* 130 no.2 (January 11, 1992): 27-30.

Meisel, Alan and Marc Kuczewski. "Legal and Ethical Myths About Informed Consent," *Archives of Internal Medicine.* 156 no.22 (December 1996): 2521-2526.

Meyer, E. Kathryn. USP Veterinary Practitioners' Reporting Program: Program Information and Case Studies," Presentation before the American Association of Feline Practitioners (AAFP) in Nashville, TN on October 19, 1999.

Miller, Neil Z. *Vaccines: Are They Really Safe and Effective?* Santa Fe, NM: New Atlantean Press, 1993 (updated in 2003).

Miller, Neil Z. *Immunization: Theory vs. Reality: Exposé on Vaccinations.* Santa Fe, NM: New Atlantean Press, 1996.

Minor, R. "Clinical Rabies of Possible Vaccinal Origin in Two Dogs," *The Veterinary Record.* 99 no.9 (August 28, 1976):173-174.

Mori, Takeshi, Yeon-Sil Shin, Masatsugu Okita, Norio Hirayama, Naoko Miyashita, Tsuyoshi Gemma, Chieko Kai and Takeshi Mikami. "The Biological Characterization of Field Isolates of Canine Distemper Virus from Japan," *Journal of General Virology.* 75 (pt 9.) (September 1994): 2403-2408.

Mori, Takeshi, Yeon-Sil Shin, Masatsugu Okita, Norio Hirayama, Naoko Miyashita, Tsuyoshi Gemma, Chieko Kai and Takeshi Mikami. "The Biological Characterization of Field Isolates of Canine Distemper Virus from Japan," *Journal of General Virology.* 75 no.11 (November 1994): 3285.

Mullin, Derek J. and R. Glen Boswall. "Comments on *Hollis v. Birch*," In *Products Liability in Canada,* 339-355. Toronto: Insight Press, 1996.

Murray, Jerry. "Injection-Site Sarcomas in a Ferret," *Journal of the American Veterinary Medical Association.* 213 no.7 (October 1, 1998): 955.

Narang, H. K. "Efficacy of Herpes Vaccine in a Rabbit Model Following Intraocular Inoculation of Herpes Simplex Virus," *Journal of Infectious*

Diseases. 149 no.6 (June 1984): 973-979.

Narang, H. K. "Scrapie, an Unconventional Virus: The Current Views," Proceedings of the Society for Experimental Biology and Medicine 184 (1987): 375-388.

Narang, H. K. "Open Letter to Tony Blair MP from Dr. Harash Narang, (April 2, 2001), http://www.cjdfoundation.com/letter.htm

Narang, H. K. "Lingering Doubts about Spongiform Encephalopathy and Creutzfeldt-Jacob Disease," *Experimental Biology and Medicine*. 226 (July 2001): 640-652.

National Advisory Committee on Immunization. *Canadian Immunization Guide*. Ottawa: Canadian Medical Association, 1998.

O'Connor, Thomas P., Quentin J. Tonelli and Janet M. Scarlett. "Report of the National FeLV/FIV Awareness Project," *Journal of the American Veterinary Medical Association*. 199 no.10 (November 15, 1991): 1348-1353.

Okoh, A. E. J. "Canine Rabies in Nigeria, 1970-1980 Reported Cases in Vaccinated Dogs," *International Journal of Zoonoses*. 9 no.2 (December 1982): 118-125.

Olsen, Christopher W. "A Review of Feline Infectious Peritonitis Virus: Molecular Biology, Immunopathogenesis, Clinical Aspects, and Vaccination," *Veterinary Microbiology*. 36 (1993): 1-37.

Orr, C. M. and C. J. Gaskell. "Interaction of an Intranasal Combined Feline Viral Rhinotracheitis, Feline Calicivirus and the FVR Carrier State," *The Veterinary Record*. (February 23, 1980), 164-166.

Parish, H. J. *Victory With Vaccines: The Story of Immunization*. Edinburgh: E. S. Livingstone Ltd., 1968.

Parrish, Colin. "Host Range Relationships and the Evolution of Canine Parvovirus," *Veterinary Microbiology*. 69 no. 1-2 (1000): 29-40.

Pedersen, Niels C., Richard W. Emmons, Robert Selcer, James D. Woodie, Terril A. Holliday and Max Weiss. "Rabies Vaccine Virus Infection in Three Dogs," *Journal of the American Veterinary Medical Association*. 172 no.9 (May 1, 1978): 1092-1096.

Pedersen, N. C. and J. F. Boyle. "Immunologic Phenomena in the Effusive Form of Feline Infectious Peritonitis," *American Journal of Veterinary Research*. 41 no.6 (June 1980): 868-876.

Pederson, N. C. and J. W. Black. "Attempted Immunization of Cats Against Feline Infectious Peritonitis Using Avirulent Live Virus or Sublethal Amounts of Virulent Virus," *American Journal of Veterinary Research*. 44 no.2 (February 1983): 229-234.

Pederson, Niels C. and Richard L. Ott. "Evaluation of a Commercial Feline Leukemia Virus Vaccine for Immunogenicity and Efficacy," *Feline Practice*. 15 no.6 (November-December 1985): 7-20.

Pederson, Niels C., J. B. Elliott, A. Glasgow, A. Poland and K. Keel. "An Isolated Epizootic of Haemorrhagic-Like Fever in Cats Caused by a Novel and Highly Virulent Strain of Feline Calicivirus," *Veterinary Microbiology*. 73 no.4 (May 2000): 281-300.

Philipson, L., U. Pettersson and U. Lindberg. "Molecular Biology of Adenoviruses," *Virology Monographs*. Vol. 14 Wein: Springer-Verlag, 1975.

Pitcairn, Richard H. and Susan Hubble Pitcairn. *Dr. Pitcairn's Complete Guide to Natural Health for Dogs & Cats.* Emmaus, PA: Rodale Press, Inc., 1995.

Plotkin, Stanley A. and Hilary Koprowski. "Rabies Vaccine," in *Vaccines.* ed. Edward A. Mortimer and Stanley A. Plotkin., 649-670. Philadelphia W.B. Saunders Co., 1994.

Pollock, Roy V. and Leland E. Carmichael. "Dog Response to Inactivated Canine Parvovirus and Feline Panleukopenia Virus Vaccines," *Cornell Vet.* 72 (1982): 16-35.

Pollock, R. V. H. and L. E. Carmichael. "Maternally Derived Immunity to Canine Parvovirus Infection: Transfer, Decline, and Interference with Vaccination," *Journal of the American Veterinary Medical Association.* 180 no.1 (January 1, 1982): 37-42.

Pollock, Roy V. and Keith N. Haffer. "Review of the First Feline Leukemia Virus Vaccine," *Journal of the American Veterinary Medical Association.* 199 no.10 (November 15, 1991): 1406-1409.

Radford, A. D., S. Dawson, C. Wharmby, R. Ryvar and R. M. Gaskell. "Comparison of Serological and Sequence-Based Methods for Typing Feline Calicivirus Isolates from Vaccine Failures," *The Veterinary Record.* (January 29, 2000): 117-123.

Reeves, N. C. Postorino, R. V. H. Pollock and E. T. Thurber. "Long-Term Follow-Up Study of Cats Vaccinated with a Temperature-Sensitive Feline Infectious Peritonitis Vaccine," *Cornell Vet.* 82 (1992): 117-123.

Rentko, Virginia T., Nancy Clark, Linda A. Ross and Scott H. Schelling. "Canine Leptospirosis: A Retrospective Study of 17 Cases," *Journal of Veterinary Internal Medicine.* 6 no.4 (1992): 235-244.

Ritter, Joseph. "Immunosuppression with Combined Vaccines," *Journal of the American Veterinary Medical Association.* 182 no.11 (June 1, 1983): 1160f.

Rohrbach, Barton W., Alfred M. Legendre, Charles A. Baldwin, Donald H. Lein, Willie M. Reed and Ronald B. Wilson. "Epidemiology of Feline Infectious Peritonitis among Cats at Veterinary Medical Teaching Hospitals," *Journal of the American Veterinary Medical Association.* 218 no.7 (April 1, 2001): 1111-1115.

Rojko, Jennifer L. and Gary J. Kociba. "Pathogenesis of Infection by the Feline Leukemia Virus," *Journal of the American Veterinary Medical Association.* 199 no.10 (November 15, 1991): 1305-1309.

Rook, A. W. and Alimuddin Zumla. "Gulf War Syndrome: Is it Due to a Systemic Shift in Cytokine Balance Towards a Th2 Profile?" *Lancet.* 349 (June 21, 1997): 1831-1833.

Ross, Linda A. "Leptospirosis," In *Kirk's Current Veterinary Therapy XIII: Small Animal Practice.* ed. John D. Bonagura, 308-310. Philadelphia: W. B. Saunders Co., 2000.

Rupprecht, Charles E. and James E. Childs. "Feline Rabies," *Feline Practice.* 24 no.5 (September/October 1996): 15-19.

Sandler, Ian, Mark Teeger and Susan Best. "Metastatic Vaccine-Associated Fibrosarcoma in a 10-Year-Old Cat," *Canadian Veterinary Journal.* 38 (June 1997): 374.

Schell, Ronald. "OspA Induces Lyme Arthritis in Hamsters," [Abstract]

Paper presented at the 12th Annual Lyme Disease Foundation Scientific Conference, New York City, New York, April 9, 1999.

Schultz, Ronald D. "Theoretical and Practical Aspects of an Immunization Program for Dogs and Cats," *Journal of the American Veterinary Medical Association.* 181 no. 10 (November 15, 1982): 1142-1149.

Schultz, R. D. "Duration of Immunity to Canine Vaccines: What We Know and Don't Know," In *Canine Infectious Diseases: From Clinics to Molecular Pathogenesis.* ed. L. Carmichael, document no. P0177.0899. Ithaca: International Veterinary Information Service, 1999. www.ivis.org

Scott, Fred W. "Evaluation of Risks and Benefits Associated with Vaccination Against Coronavirus Infections in Cats," In *Advances in Veterinary Medicine.* Vol. 41., ed. Ronald D. Schultz, 347-358. San Diego: Academic Press, 1999.

Scott, Fred W. and Cordell M. Geissinger. "Long-Term Immunity in Cats Vaccinated with an Inactivated Trivalent Vaccine," *American Journal of Veterinary Research.* 60 no.5 (May 1999): 652-658.

Sharp, N. J., B. J. Davis, J. S. Guy, J. M. Cullen, S. F. Steingold and J. N. Kornegay. "Hydranencephaly and Cerebellar Hypoplasia in Two Kittens Attributed to Intrauterine Parvovirus Infection," *Journal of Comparative Pathology.* 121 no.1 (July 1999): 39-53.

Siegl, Günter. "Canine Parvoviruses: Origin and Significance of a 'New' Pathogen," In *The Parvoviruses.* ed. Kenneth I. Berns, 363-388. New York: Plenum Press, 1984.

Sigal, Leonard H. "Lyme Disease: A Review of Aspects of Its Immunology and Immuno-pathogenesis," *Annual Reviews of Immunology.* 15 no.1 (1997): 63-92.

Starr, Robin M. "Reaction Rate in Cats Vaccinated with a New Controlled-Titer Feline Panleukopenia-Rhinotracheitis-calicivirus-*Chlamydia Psittaci* Vaccine," *Cornell Vet.* 83 no.4 (1993): 311-323.

Sturgess, C. P., T. J. Gruffydd-Jones, D. A. Harbour and H. R. Feilden. "Studies on the Safety of *Chlamydia Psittaci* Vaccination in Cats," *The Veterinary Record.* 137 no.26 (December 23/30 1995): 668-669.

Summers, B. A., H. A. Greisen and M. J. G. Appel. "Possible Initiation of Viral Encephalomyelitis in Dogs by Migrating Lymphocytes Infected with Distemper Virus," *The Lancet.* 2 no. 8082 (July 22, 1978): 187-189.

Tizard, Ian. "Grease, Anthraxgate, and Kennel Cough: A Revisionist History of Early Veterinary Vaccines," In *Advances in Veterinary Medicine* Vol. 41., ed. Ronald D. Schultz, 7-24. San Diego: Academic Press, 1999.

Tizard, Ian and Edmund P. Bass. "Evaluation of a Killed, Whole Virion Feline Leukemia Virus Vaccine," *Journal of the American Veterinary Medical Association.* 199 no.10 (November 15, 1991): 1410-1413.

Toshach, Katrina, Mark W. Jackson and Richard S. Dubielzig. "Hepatocellular Necrosis Associated with the Subcutaneous Injection of an Intranasal Brodetella Bronchiseptica-Canine Parainfluenza Vaccine," *J. of the American Animal Hospital.* 33 (March/April 1997): 126-128.

Tratschin, Jon-Duri, Gary K. McMaster, Gurtrud Kronauer and Günter Seigl. "Canine Parvovirus: Relationsjip to Wild-type and Vaccine Strains of Feline Panleukopenia Virus and Mink Enteritis Virus," *Journal of General Virology.* 61 Pt. 1 (1982): 33-41.

Truyen, U. "Emergence and Recent Evolution of Canine Parvovirus," *Veterinary Microbiology.* 69 no. 1-2 (1999): 47-50.

Venemma, H., R. J. de Groot, D. A. Harbour, M. Dalderup, T. Gruffydd-Jones, M. C. Horzinek and W. J. Spaan. "Early Death after Feline Infectious Peritonitis Virus Challenge Due to Recombinant Vaccinia Virus Immunization," *J. of Virology.* 64 no.3 (March 1990): 1407-1409.

Vennema, Harry, Amy Poland, Janet Foley and Niels C. Pederson. "Feline Infectious Peritonitis Viruses Arise by Mutation from Endemic Feline Enteric Coronaviruses," *Virology.* 243 no.1 (March 30, 1998): 150-157.

Vermint SIRI, MSDS, http://hazard.com/msds/tox/f/q14/q785.html

Verschoor, Ernst J., Marja J. Willemse, Jeanette G. Stam, Arno L. W. van Vliet, Henk Pouwels, Stuart K. Chalmers, Marian C. Horzinek, Paul J. A. Sondermeijer, Wim Hesselink and Anthony de Ronde. "Evaluation of Subunit Vaccines Against Feline Immunodeficiency Virus Infection," *Vaccine.* 14 no.4 (1996): 285-289.

Wagener, Jeffrey S., Richard Sobonya, Linda Minnich and Lynn M. Taussig. "Role of Canine Parainfluenza Virus and Bordetella Bronchiseptica in Kennel Cough," *American Journal of Veterinary Research.* 45 no.9 (September 1984): 1862-1866.

Wardley, R. "Vaccines for Cats," In *Veterinary Vaccinology.* e.d. P. P. Pastoret et al., 336-339. Amsterdam: Elsevier Science B.V., 1997.

Wilbur, Linn A., James F. Evermann, Randall L. Levings, Ione R. Stoll, David E. Starling, Carol A. Spillers, Gary A. Gustafson and Alison J. McKiernan. "Abortion and Death in Pregnant Bitches Associated with Bluetongue Virus," *Journal of the American Veterinary Medical Association.* 204 no.11 (June 1, 1994): 1762-1765.

Wilcock, Brian P. and Julie A. Yager. "Focal Cutaneous Vasculitis and Alopecia at Site of Rabies Vaccination in Dogs," *Journal of the American Veterinary Medical Association.* 188 no.10 (May 15, 1986): 1174-1177.

Willemse, Marja J., Saskia H. B. van Schooneveld, W. Stuart K. Chalmers and Paul J. A. Sondermeijer. "Vaccination Against Feline Leukemia Using a New Feline Herpes Virus Type 1 Vector," *Vaccine.* 14 no.16 (1996): 1511-1516.

Wilson, Sir Graham S. *Hazards of Immunization.* London: The Athelone Press, 1967.

Wilson, R. B., C. E. Kord, J. A. Holladay and J. S. Cave. "A Neurologic Syndrome Associated with Use of Canine Coronavirus-Parvovirus Vaccine in Dogs," *The Compendium on Continuing Education for the Practicing Veterinarian.* 8 no.2 (February 1986): 117-124.

Wolf, Alice M. "Feline Infectious Peritonitis: Part 2," *Feline Practice.* 25 no.3 (May/June 1997): 24-28.

Yazbak, F. E. "Maternal Vaccination and Autism," Paper presented at the International Public Conference on Vaccination 2000, Arlington, VA, (September 10, 2000).

Yokoyama, N., K. Maeda, Y. Tohya, Y. Kawaguchi, K. Fujita and T. Mikami. "Recombinant Feline Herpesvirus Type 1 Expressing Immunologic Proteins Inducible Virus Neutralizing Antibody Against Feline Calicivirus in Cats," *Vaccine.* 14 no.17/18 (1996): 1657-1663.

Index

About the Author

Catherine J. M. Diodati, MA, is a vaccine expert, legal consultant, and biomedical ethicist. She began researching vaccines in 1985 following her daughter's near-fatal reaction to her third set of vaccinations.

Catherine attended King's College, London, and the University of Windsor, where she received her Bachelor of Arts, Honors degree in 1995. Her undergraduate work focused on philosophy, theology, and ethics. Upon graduation, Catherine received the Board of Governor's Medal for academic excellence. Catherine received her Master's Degree from the University of Windsor in 1998. Her postgraduate research focused on biomedical ethics and mass vaccination. Her Master's Thesis, *Biomedical Ethics: The Ethics Implications of Mass Immunization*, was successfully defended before a team of experts in Biomedical Ethics, Immunology, Nursing, and Law. As a result, her research was requested to be incorporated in Biology courses at the University of Windsor and as part of the restructuring of Cancer Care Ontario. During her postgraduate research, Catherine received the Assumption University Scholarship. She was the first student ever to have received the University of Windsor Scholarship and the Ontario Graduate Scholarship simultaneously. Catherine was selected as a candidate for the Governor General's Medal. Selections for this award are limited to the top achieving student in each discipline.

Following graduation, Catherine published *Immunization: History, Ethics, Law and Health* (1999). This publication was groundbreaking because it was the first to examine vaccination in depth from a bioethical perspective. Her research culminated in an extensive review of mass vaccination in terms of non-maleficence, beneficence, respect for autonomy (informed and voluntary consent), and justice. She examined the history of vaccine development, vaccine production, the safety of vaccine components (i.e. host tissues, chemicals, antigens), the historical efficacy of vaccines, adverse events, compensation for vaccine-injuries, and new vaccines under development.

Catherine now travels internationally to provide professional, often accredited, and lay presentations on vaccination. For example, she recently offered a formal presentation for the International Chiropractors' Association International Conference on Chiropractic and Pediatrics. She has also provided vaccine research and interviews for several newspapers, television, and radio programs. Catherine has published a number of articles on vaccination. Her work has appeared in the *Canadian Medical Association Journal, Canadian Chiropractor,* and several other medical and vaccine-associated journals. A new article, written in conjunction with Dr. F. Edward Yazbak, appears in the August 2002 issue of *Medical Hypotheses.* She also published a booklet entitled *Flu Shots: What You Need to Know Before Making a Decision* (2000), which challenges the influenza vaccine mandate imposed upon Ontario Health Care Workers. The challenge is based upon The Canadian Charter of Rights and Freedoms and The Ontario Health Care Consent Act, which have been violated by the mandate. The arguments presented have become the central issue of a case presently being reviewed by The Ontario Superior Court of Justice.

Catherine has also been consulted when vaccination has become an issue in schools, for child custody, military transfers, immigration, social services, and employment. Ongoing cases in which Catherine's expertise has been called upon include: *The State of Florida v. Alan Raymond Yurko* (Case No. CR98-1730); *Toronto Civic Employees Union, Local 416 v. The Attorney General of Ontario and The City of Toronto* (Court File 156/2001); and, *Bill Kotsopoulos v. North Bay General Hospital* (Court File No.2316/02).

Catherine is a former President and current Area Governor of Toastmasters. She lives in Windsor, Ontario with her 18-year-old daughter Ashleigh and three-year-old black and white cat Benjamin. Her pets have included an English sheepdog, a Beagle, an English bull terrier, and a Tuxedo cat. Catherine is particularly fond of cats, dogs, and horses.

Purchasing Information

Additional copies of **Vaccine Guide for Dogs and Cats: What Every Pet Lover Should Know** (ISBN: 1-881217-34-5) may be purchased directly from *New Atlantean Press*. Call 505-983-1856. Or send $13.95 (in U.S. funds), plus $3.50 shipping, to:

New Atlantean Press
PO Box 9638
Santa Fe, NM 87504
505-983-1856 (Telephone & Fax)
Email: global@thinktwice.com

This book is also available at many bookstores and health stores: 1-881217-34-5.

Bookstores and Retail Buyers: Order from Baker & Taylor, Ingram, Midpoint, New Leaf, Nutri-Books, or from New Atlantean Press. Libraries may order this book from Quality Books, Unique Books, or from your favorite library wholesaler.

Veterinarians, Homeopaths, Animal Breeders, Vaccine Organizations, and other Non-Storefront Buyers: Take a 40% discount with the purchase of 5 or more copies (multiply the total cost of purchases x .60). Please add 7% ($3.50 minimum) for shipping.

Shipping: Please add 7% ($3.50 minimum) for shipping. Allow one to three weeks for your order to arrive, or include $3.00 extra for priority air mail shipping. **Foreign orders** must include 20% ($5.50 minimum) for shipping. Air mail is available. Please email us for rates: global@thinktwice.com Checks must be drawn on a U.S.A. bank, or send a Postal Money Order in U.S.A. funds. **Sales Tax:** Please add 6% for books shipped to New Mexico addresses.

Vaccines: Are They *Really* Safe and Effective? (ISBN: 1-881217-30-2) by Neil Z. Miller. This bestselling vaccine handbook (over 100,000 copies sold!) evaluates each vaccine for safety, efficacy, and long-term effects. It contains the most comprehensive, up-to-date, uncensored data available— information that many doctors don't even know. It includes the most recent studies, numerous case histories detailing vaccine-induced damage to children, and pinpoints for parents exact conditions that may put their own child at high risk. It includes information on vaccine ingredients, natural versus artificial immunity, and provides data documenting correlations between MMR and autism, polio vaccines and cancer, the hepatitis B vaccine and multiple sclerosis, the Hib vaccine and diabetes, and much more. In addition, it outlines current vaccine laws and offers parental options to "mandatory" shots. This book is available at many bookstores and health stores. You may also order from the publisher: **New Atlantean Press**, PO Box 9638, Santa Fe, NM 87504. Call **505-983-1856** to order by credit card.

FREE CATALOG: *New Atlantean Press* offers the world's largest selection of uncensored vaccine information, including up-to-date vaccine laws, vaccine books, and other hard-to-find vaccine resources. We also offer numerous books on cutting-edge alternative health solutions, natural immunity, progressive parenting, holistic childcare, healing disease, and more. Send for a free catalog: *New Atlantean Press,* PO Box 9638, Santa Fe, NM 87504. Or visit the:

Thinktwice Global Vaccine Institute
www.thinktwice.com